PHIL ROSS

ONCE A TROJAN, ALWAYS A TROJAN

ONCE A TROJAN

ALWAYS A TROJAN

A TRUE STORY

PHIL ROSS

Preface

By JOE OBBEMA

FIRST EDITION

Library of Congress Cataloging-in-Publication Data has been applied for.

ISBN 13: 978-1484951224

ISBN 10: 1484951220

Dedicated to the Memory of

A Great Football Coach,

Jim Erkenbeck

ONCE A TROJAN, ALWAYS A TROJAN

TABLE OF CONTENTS

PREFACE

When I was asked to write this Preface by Phil Ross, a former longtime sportswriter in Southern California, Nevada, Texas and Colorado, I was enthused. He did an incredible job of over 50 hours of interviews and tapings including myself, my teammates, coaches and my family. He also interviewed some world-class athletes and Hall of Famers such as Ron Yary, the Outland Trophy winner in 1967 as the nation's best college lineman and Tim Rossovich, an All-American and a first-round draft choice by the Philadelphia Eagles; baseball players like Fernando Valenzuela, Maury Wills and Tommy Davis; and Mike Garrett, the 1964 Heisman Trophy winner for the University of Southern California. Also interviewed were former College and NFL head coaches such as Wayne Fontes, Jim Fassel and Jim Hanifan, all friends of mine from various stages of my life and playing career.

I thought long and hard about what I wanted to say about this book. The first thing that I want to make clear is that this is not just about the 1967 national championship team that included a Heisman Trophy winner, Outland Trophy winner, five first-round NFL draft choices and a total of nine All-Americans. It is about family, parenthood, and handling challenging and difficult times, no matter who you are, where you come from or where you're going.

To begin with, there is something that "Mr. Trojan", Nick Pappas, told me before I entered USC. He said that "You can be a UCLA Bruin for four years or a USC Trojan for a lifetime." I chose to be a USC Trojan and had no idea how true that is and how much it would affect my family, life and my business career. The bond I formed with my teammates, coaches and the university is still prevalent today. It helped me get through difficult times such as anorexia that reduced my first wife to 67 pounds before she would let me get her help, and the death of my fianceé Maureen just six weeks before our wedding. The accidental death of my younger brother Bobby at age 32 coupled with the unexpected death of one of my sisters at age 57 were other tragedies discussed in the book, along with my own near-death experience and my patriotic mother's untimely passing the day after 9-11.

The bond that I formed was so strong that it got me through life and helped me succeed in business as well. For instance, as the book details, I began to organize a charity golf tournament with my good friend Scott Crane and convinced many friends, aforementioned former teammates and coaches and other sports and entertainment celebrities to play annually. Through my characteristic persistence, they helped make the annual event a success and we were able to raise approximately $200,000 over the course of 10 years.

These funds went to a charity called SAFE, Southern Area Foster Care Effort. The money provided college scholarships and medical directories for services for foster children and their loving foster parents.

This same bond has further helped me and my second wife of 25 years, Linda, to raise seven children and has given us eight wonderful and loving grandchildren.

In closing, I would like to tell you what my Mater Dei High School coach Dick Coury said before every game. It was impactful for life. I have paraphrased the maxim and it simply goes like this:

"If you think you're beaten, you are. If you think you are not, you don't. If you would like to win but think you can't, it's almost a cinch you won't. For in this life you'll find life's battles don't always go to the biggest or strongest man but sooner or later they go to the fellow who thinks he can."

Dick Coury's words and the bond I have formed with the University of Southern California helped me in every aspect of my life. Please enjoy this book and remember that tough times don't last but tough people do.

PROLOGUE

To this day, in the whole, wide world, there are only 68 people, living and dead – 58 players and 10 coaches – who share the truly unique honor of having earned a certain, special piece of gold jewelry encased with a cardinal-colored stone and their names or initial engraved on the inside.

That showpiece is the ring denoting the University of Southern California 1967 football team's achievement as consensus national champion.

Among those 68 are two dual Hall-of-Famers (College Football and Pro Football) whose lives have taken greatly divergent paths. One double Hall of Fame electee is legendary tailback and future Heisman Award winner O.J. Simpson, who received a different type notoriety later in life away from the football field; the other is towering offensive tackle Ron Yary, who won the Outland Trophy that championship season as the nation's top interior lineman and then toiled in the trenches for 15 seasons, mostly with the Minnesota Vikings, garnering All-Pro recognition eight times.

But also among the elite 68 Trojan ring-bearers from '67 is a tenacious, likable and quick-witted defensive lineman, linebacker and occasional fullback named Joe Obbema, who has his own special story to tell – one about life, not just football.

1

SNAPPING THE JINX OF THE IRISH

He turned him right and round about Upon the Irish shore;

And gae his handle reins a shake,With adieu forevermore,

My dear – And adieu forevermore!

-- Johnson's Musical Museum. It Was A' for Our Rightfu' King, St.3

Robert Burns (1759-1796)

The United DC8 glided through the Midwest sky, carrying the USC Trojans to a date on a faraway, yet legendary, field in northwest Indiana. An edgy 19-year-old, Joe Obbema, fidgeted with the metal controls of his seat, which seemed too small for his huge hands and 6-foot-2, 225-pound frame.

"I was nervous; we all were nervous, but we all had a single goal in mind," Obbema, now 65, admitted when looking back on that flight that happened one fall afternoon in 1967. The sole aim was to land at O'Hare International Airport in Chicago, spend a hopefully restful night in a local hotel, then take a 2 ½-hour bus ride across the Indiana state line to South Bend, arriving about three hours before game time. Once there, the collective goal was to accomplish something the University of Southern California Trojans hadn't done on the football field since 1939: Beat the defending national champion Notre Dame Fighting Irish on the road.

For Obbema, this was his first-ever airplane trip outside of traveling to the six other Pacific-8 Conference schools not located in Los Angeles.

The sleek jet was occupied in the usual manner as was customary on USC road trips. The same flight crew that had staffed the team's charters for years was on board. In the first-class section sat alumni, administrators and others who did not play or coach, but who were able to whoop and holler, and have a grand time.

Just behind the partition in the first row of the coach cabin relaxing side-by-side were wry, witty and often-profane Head Coach John McKay and his *ad hoc* assistant head coach, bookish, easy-going offensive line coach Dave Levy. While McKay was most comfortable with a cigar – lit or unlit – dangling from his mouth, Levy's tastes ran to non-fiction books such as history or biography volumes.

Immediately in back of McKay and Levy – and wound up as usual like a tightly knit ball of yarn just before a cat dug its paws into it – was crew-cut, dark-eyed assistant coach Marv Goux. Goux was "The Spirit of the Trojans," as fellow USC assistant Dick Coury had described his colleague. Goux, who passed away in 2002, a year after McKay, was the individual who could be counted on to take it upon himself to exhort the troops with impassioned speeches, whether merely in practice or a tense locker-room setting. "When it was time for some really fiery pep talks, (Goux) would take over," stated star tailback O.J. Simpson in his autobiographical 1970 book, *O.J.: The Education Rich Rookie*, on which he collaborated with Pete Axthelm. "Coach McKay would give a fight talk, and then Coach Goux would take over and really go at it – and we'd go out for the second half ready to tear somebody apart."

Said the longtime Voice of the Trojans, Tom Kelly, "(Goux) served a very important function for McKay," that of a "bad cop" who took it upon himself to be chief chider of the players while McKay quietly chuckled that he did not have to perform that function.

The rest of the aptly named "coach" section was filled with other assistant coaches plus Obbema and the other 60-odd players on the traveling squad. Rather than partying like those up front, each of the *actual* combatants had his own intensely personal ritual – or none at all – in coping with the mounting tension that accompanies the eventual butting of helmets when two of the nation's top football squads meet annually.

"I tried not to think too much about it, except for the plays and the history of it," said junior defensive lineman Bill Hayhoe, one of the quietest Trojans who tacitly let his on-field performance do most of his "talking."

Left guard Steve Lehmer, the only sophomore who started on offense that season, used a specific upper-class line mate as his own personal sounding board. Any time Lehmer wanted advice and consolation, he would turn to center Dick Allmon, who in his mind was the most approachable of the experienced teammates.

"(Being) the only starting sophomore on offense . . . I was kind of the little kid on offense,"

Lehmer said. "I was in awe of 'Troy', kind of in awe of (seniors Mike) Taylor, (Mike) Scarpace and (Ron) Yary, so the only one I felt I could talk to was Allmon," the articulate starting junior center who always lined up immediately to Lehmer's right. "He had a calming effect."

Then there was that other sophomore teammate, Joe Obbema. He did not know it then, but Obbema, a young man with a billy-goat-gruff exterior yet a soft-as-lamb's-wool heart, had embarked on the early part of a much longer and meaningful journey. During that sometimes arduous, lifelong trek, he would come to be regarded often by most of those around him as someone who was fiercely loyal, trustworthy and always went out of his way to stand up for the less-fortunate. Even long after his football career ended, Obbema could be counted on, whether to console or protect friends, family or even strangers.

"Someone asked me why I can do this, and I said because I can," admitted Obbema, one of only a handful of sophomores who had earned their way onto the active roster of the team, which was No. 1 in the nation and carrying a 4-0 record into the Notre Dame confrontation. There were only 18 freshmen in his entering class the previous year in 1966, and National Collegiate Athletic Association regulations forbade them from playing on the varsity until they were sophomores; they practiced daily with the varsity.

Prior to that '67 season, one day when the freshmen were coming off the field from the final preseason "double-day" drills, Obbema said that classmate and linebacker Bob Jensen turned to him and said, as he extended his hand, 'Well, we made it, buddy.' But until he received official word from the coaches, Obbema said he still was not totally certain, even though he had an underlying, yet quiet, confidence. "It never occurred to me that I wasn't gonna make the team. It would've broken my heart."

Only nine of that group remained by the '67 game against the Irish, of which Obbema said, "Being No. 1 at the time . . . we wanted to keep that status and win a national championship" on a senior- and junior-dominated team. He spent most of the season either as a regular on special teams or in the fourth quarter of most games as a stand-up defensive end spelling senior All-America and future NFL starter Tim Rossovich in a 5-2 alignment.

"Coach McKay had been embarrassed, and he stressed the importance of beating Notre Dame after the 51-0 loss to them at home the previous year," he said. "(For) the players, believe me, revenge was on (our) minds. At the end of each practice that season leading up to the Notre Dame game, we devoted 15 minutes specifically to running Notre Dame plays."

Obbema then mentioned the hostile environment at Notre Dame Stadium that was exacerbated by a tunnel through which both teams entered the field of combat. "There had always been some sort of confrontation" in the past within the narrow confines of the tunnel, he said.

However, before that there was another hurdle of sorts to overcome – one for which the younger Trojans had been given due notice.

Irish fans ringed the Chicago hotel where the Trojans stayed with a "motorcade" to greet the visitors. Obbema's roommate on this trip was fellow defensive player, and the only sophomore defensive starter, Jimmy Gunn. Despite the doings below, Obbema said, "Neither of us had trouble sleeping. I don't know how long they stayed out there, but we went to sleep around midnight."

Obviously not too many other Men of Troy had sleepless nights either, as evidenced by the results the next day, although Lehmer admitted to being bothered by the attendant hubbub. *He* did not sleep well that night. "There were both older and younger people – they were as nasty as they could be," said Lehmer, who went on to become an orthopedic surgeon and today works as a consulting surgeon in Northern California.

"I didn't remember any noise from my room but I heard about it," said the 6-8, 265-pound Hayhoe. "The cops tried to get things settled down," the tall defensive lineman said. He knew a lot about cops since his 93-year-old father, Bill, Sr., retired after 29 years as a Los Angeles police officer to grow dry-land almonds on his small parcel along the Central California coast.

The revelers were the age of college students in some cases, but also included Irish fans who were in their 50s or 60s.

"I thought it was a parade, just being around the hotel and circling it with cymbals, drums, trumpets and music. They tried to keep our players awake," said USC assistant offensive line coach Rod Humenuik, who now lives in Scottsdale, Ariz., with wife Susie. He remembered that it was after midnight – in other words, well past curfew on the eve of a game.

"We went out – some of the coaches went out" to ensure the Trojan players would not become personally involved with the "paraders" and that the team would have a decent wake-up about 6 or 7 a.m., Humenuik said.

Obbema was more nervous for that game than any previous one. But he had solace to calm the nervousness in a great-aunt who lived in the Chicago area. "She really wanted to talk to me," he said. But the older relative had been informed that family members could not see players before the game, yet she persisted by phoning frequently until able to see her nephew. The aunt's resolute attitude was evident in the Obbema bloodlines, something her grand-nephew himself would carry with him forever, football or not, in episode after episode of a decidedly colorful life – on and off the field.

"Coach Goux said she kept calling the front desk every five minutes and was very persistent, so I got to spend 15 minutes with her. He told me, 'Go and talk with her, but don't take too long, and get your butt back in here to get some rest,'" he added. All this was more remarkable since everyone connected with USC knew that Goux was *the* ultimate intimidator – until, of course, he encountered Joe Obbema's great-aunt, and was forced to give in.

Dick Coury and the rest of the Trojan coaching stuff were none-too-surprised by this self-discipline exhibited by their charges, especially young Obbema, prior to the game. Coury was head coach at Mater Dei High School, a coeducational Catholic institution in Santa Ana, the county seat of suburban Orange County, about 30 miles southeast of the USC campus, throughout Obbema's prep career. So Coury knew the tough youngster as well as anyone.

"He didn't waste time in a crisis situation. He was one of the leaders . . . He was always prepared because of practice," said Coury, who later was a longtime National Football League assistant for several teams as well as head coach at Cal State Fullerton and the since-defunct World Football League and United States Football League.

Coury, who had coached many outstanding players at Mater Dei and USC including Notre Dame's 1964 Heisman winner, quarterback John Huarte, said Obbema possessed among the best attitudes and set of leadership credentials of anyone he had ever mentored.

Like Lehmer, Obbema and his fellow sophomores also were prepared for the Notre Dame partisans' "shillelagh shenanigans" with the counsel of the more-veteran players. One, ironically, was Ireland-born senior linebacker Adrian Young, like Obbema a Southland parochial product (Bishop Amat in suburban La Puente).

Young, as was the case with Northern California native Rossovich, who also was a Catholic high school graduate, would go on to be drafted in the first round and play in the NFL for several years. Long before the hotel incident, the former advised Obbema on the plane trip halfway across the country of what to expect from the time they landed until after the game was over.

As assistant coaches walked up and down the aisle after the "Fasten Seat Belts" light had been turned off, they would witness various activities on the players' parts. Over here were a couple of edgy sophomores trying to break the tenseness by playing a no-stakes poker game with an older teammate or two; over there were seatmates snoring loudly as they dozed off, oblivious to anyone around them.

The older players had warned the younger ones well ahead of time, based on firsthand experience. "The seniors had been back there two years before when they were sophomores, and had lost," Obbema said. He said Young "kind of took me under his wing . . . He would tell you things. I would always ask what to expect. On the plane, I would play cards with him, Gunn and some other guys, and I'd ask a lot of questions."

Then, following their arrival at the hotel, there was a team meeting in which the warning about any potential disruption by the Fighting Irish "welcoming party" was a key topic. In the meeting, despite the reassurances, the younger Trojans persisted with questions about what to anticipate, never totally shaking their nervousness. While Rossovich and Young were two distinctly different personalities, they were in harmony in calming underclassmen's qualms.

Levy remembers Rossovich, a serious prankster off the football field, as "never a problem on the field or academically. He was extremely respectful to the coaches. He did things away from football to get attention.

"Adrian was much more the golden-boy type – a good student and player," Levy added. "The Notre Dame game certainly was something that would make or break our season," said Rossovich, now in his mid-60s, and proprietor, with his wife, Lauren, of a multi-faceted dog rescue and placement operation in Northern California's Sierra Nevada foothills. "The year after the embarrassment of losing 51-0 at the Coliseum" made it "a great opportunity for us. There was a lot of pressure, anxiety and concern," said Rossovich, who changed years ago from pursuing passers to chasing canines.

As for the young Obbema, he had been an exemplary running back at California's most competitive level, scoring 19 touchdowns his senior year at Mater Dei. "(He was) good enough to play both ways at SC, but McKay wouldn't let him . . . and I agreed with him," Coury said of his prize pupil.

"Joe was responsible, with his (Mater Dei) performance, for (tacitly) convincing McKay to bring in Coury," said Chuck Dekeado, a close McKay associate for many years and USC booster who conducted annual Trojan football camps.

Dekeado said Coury was hired "so we could get all those Mater Dei players at USC." (While that was partly true at the time, Coury's lifelong record as a head and assistant coach over the years bears strong testament to his ability to lead young men at every level he coached. In fact, if you ask any of his former players, they will tell you he had an unusual knack for treating them as human beings, thereby drawing the maximum performance out of these talented athletes. Senior quarterback Toby Page, who also was a Mater Dei graduate two years ahead of Obbema, said Coury also produced winners through a strong work ethic and advanced conditioning program, saying of the coach that "he just ran our butts off.")

Rossovich later went on to an acting career, including working often as *Magnum P.I.* star Tom

Selleck's double. Selleck, although not on the football team, had been Rossovich's roommate at USC for a time. Obbema's dual role as Rossovich's backup and on special teams during the 1967 season allowed him to get into games consistently on defense, as was the case at Notre Dame.

From Rossovich's perspective, viewed today through the retrospective prism of a 60-something man, his surrogate kid brother was "a wonderful young man. The relationship with him meant a lot to me then, and it means a lot to me now. Maybe I took him under my wing . . . put a hand on his shoulder and gave him a little guiding light . . . Maybe something to help him be a better player."

The senior All-America player said he felt it was his obligation to mentor younger players such as Obbema because he had been treated similarly by older players when he was younger and less experienced.

Ron Yary, the 6-foot-5, 255-pound senior offensive tackle, who would be the first overall pick in the upcoming 1968 NFL draft by the Minnesota Vikings, said he "admired those guys (the reserves and special-teams players)" even more than the starters like himself. "I was a guy who was lucky; I got to play," Yary said. (Three other members of the '67 USC team also were first-round NFL draft picks

– Rossovich, Young and wide receiver Earl McCullouch, the last a world-class hurdler and sprint-relay runner, and the *only* other player on the squad who could outrun junior tailback O.J. Simpson in a one-on-one foot race. While Simpson ran the 40-yard dash in 4.5 seconds, McCullouch was clocked at 4.4. Simpson was drafted in the first round in 1969 by Buffalo after winning the Heisman Trophy.)

"The game was always the easy part. It was fun. Practice was harder," said Yary, who went on to play 15 NFL seasons – all but one with the Vikings – and was elected both to the College Football Hall of Fame and Pro Football Hall of Fame, respectively in 1987 and 2001. He said he draws no distinction between a star player and his fellow double Hall-of-Famer, Simpson, and a hard-working role-player like Obbema – in his mind, teammates are teammates, with no one being anymore special than anyone else.

Coury had recommended and recruited Obbema, whom Levy termed as "a large and aggressive" defensive lineman "behind Rossovich, who was sort of our bell cow." (For those unfamiliar with farm lingo, a bell cow is the one bovine a dairy farmer relies upon for the other animals to follow by their adhering to the clanging bell around the lead cow's neck. However, Rossovich was such an imposing physical and emotional presence that he didn't need a bell for his teammates to follow.)

That October Saturday at Notre Dame was laid out like a film script, and that was how it was characterized by Obbema, a self-styled, devoted movie buff, who actually leans toward *Star Trek* and other science-fiction without being a hardcore Trekker himself. "Nineteen-thirty-nine, that's when (the original) *King Kong* and *Gone with the Wind* were made – the last time SC beat Notre Dame," said Obbema, who was the squad's youngest player, having just turned 19 the previous July.

The expected pre-game tunnel ruckus never materialized because McKay held back his Trojans in the relatively small locker room until the Fighting Irish stormed onto the field first, yet it was not without incident.

McKay refused to let his players rush through the tunnel until Notre Dame went out first. He wanted to avoid a confrontation because he knew the Trojans were fired up with an extra shot of adrenaline. Attributable to the extra wait, game officials told him it would be a 1-0 forfeit if USC did not enter the field on time.

Apparently, there had been a situation two years before, on USC's last visit to South Bend, when a Trojan return man received a kickoff and slipped by himself and, as a gunshot-like sound rang out, someone had yelled, "Oh, my God, they shot him."

There was a rationale in trying to avoid any mingling with the Notre Dame players. Humenuik said it was a proven strategy, and that McKay "had a good feel for tendencies. I would classify his ability, or knack, almost as a football genius."

The holding back of his players entering the field separately had its genesis back in Los Angeles, at the Coliseum, the Trojans' home stadium, where the visitors always came out first through a similar, single tunnel.

Humenuik said he thought that any "gun" sounds were likely from a small cannon that the Irish always shot off over the years in the pre-game period or after the home team scored.

"I (too) thought it was a cannon, then figured out later that it *was*," Lehmer said. He also was the target of a beer bottle as he exited the tunnel; the missile had been tossed by someone in the crowd; it hit him on a shoulder pad and bounced to the ground. "That's the way all those people were to us

– from the moment we got off the plane, to the hotel, to the field. The crowd was screaming all the time. It helped motivate all of us."

From the minute the Trojans went out onto the field, the very noisy surroundings, underscored by where Notre Dame band members sat, were noticeable.

"I didn't realize how loud it was," the then-still-nervous Obbema said of the noise generated by the gathered throng. "Other than the (annual) SC-UCLA game, it was the only time I heard the crowd." The home team's large band sat right behind the USC bench – no more than 15 yards away – and did a lot of name-calling. (No one knows whether those musicians were some of the same cymbalists, drummers and trumpeters whom Humenuik said had appeared outside the hotel in the wee hours to "serenade" his team.)

Bands indeed were irritants to reserves like the late Doug Mooers, a transfer from the Air Force Academy, standing on the sidelines waiting for the opening kickoff, even if he knew that eligibility/transfer rules would not permit him to actually enter games that season.

"Like the National Anthem – turn that fuckin' thing off, and let's play," remembered an otherwise-patriotic Mooers, a graduate of Anaheim's Western High who played three seasons in the NFL with Dallas, New Orleans and the old St. Louis Cardinals. Mooers died of bladder cancer at age 64 just before Christmas 2011 in his adopted hometown of Milwaukee, Wis., where he owned a family waste-management business.

Lehmer said the Fighting Irish players, like some of their fans, were among the most ornery he ever encountered in his college career, adding that the Notre Damers "were as nasty as it came . . . like in the pile, they were always grabbing and scratching and slugging."

That was ironic, in that Allmon was Lehmer's go-to guy among upperclassmen when it came to advice because Allmon said in the same vein that when he was a sophomore, in a road game at Miami, Fla, the host Hurricanes were similarly "dirty."

In Miami, the 'Canes players "were given free rein by their coach" to do "the physically dirtiest play I've ever seen," Allmon said. In one specific instance, the Hurricanes purposely went after Trojan punter Rich Leon, the Junior College All-American transfer from Fullerton J.C. whom Allmon described as "a fabulous natural athlete. . . Miami didn't try to block the punt; they went after him on purpose," breaking Leon's leg and ending his promising college football career.

Back at Notre Dame, the first half was uneventful and appeared to be a repeat of past USC performances in the shadow of Touchdown Jesus, the gigantic, multi-story mural astride a library wall outside one end of the stadium, as the visitors trailed, 7-0, at the half against Irish quarterback Terry Hanratty and his mates. The Trojans were able to thwart other scoring threats by the hosts and maintain the one-touchdown deficit at the midpoint.

Then something unexpected occurred on the second-half kickoff with Notre Dame set to receive the ball.

Rossovich, whom Obbema regarded as a "big brother and probably the strongest physical specimen I knew (at 6-foot-5 and 250 pounds)," kicked it. In the resultant scramble 10 yards upfield, Obbema got hold of the ball about the same time as teammate Steve Swanson, a fellow resident of suburban Buena Park, who recovered it.

Trouble was, perhaps no one else – not the coaches, *nobody* – knew about the onside kick, which led to the tying touchdown, as the Trojans decidedly assumed command of the game. By the time the winners went ahead to stay, there was an incredible "silencing" of the normally loud home crowd. When the home team falls behind for good, there is a tendency for the crowd noise to lessen naturally, especially at Notre Dame.

Propelled by the momentum provided by the surprise kick, USC rebounded to score 24 unanswered points in the second half and win, 24-7, maintaining the unbeaten, top-ranked status and, most importantly, breaking the 28-year jinx at South Bend. Simpson scored all three USC touchdowns, and rushed for 160 yards on 38 carries, much of that in the second half, as his side practiced good ball control that was characteristic of the Trojans' offense most of the season. The psychological effect of having a back like Simpson on the team was his capability of going for a touchdown any time he had the ball.

"The thing that was spectacular about O.J. was the fact that he was the only runner I ever saw that, after he was hit – once he regained his balance – he was at full speed; he'd never really take a big hit," Obbema said.

Simpson's reputation as a one-of-a-kind tailback in two seasons of junior-college ball had preceded him, and he had enhanced that on only his second play in the first USC spring practice for him and Obbema, racing 80 yards for a score. Plus, he did not fumble much.

Other than Simpson, the single other player on the USC roster capable of almost-singlehandedly changing a game was the wily Rossovich – the way star defenders like the New York Giants' Lawrence Taylor or the Baltimore Ravens' Ray Lewis would do many years later.

"Rossovich kicked extra points for us" the previous season, Humenuik said. "He was very accurate. So for him to do that (the onside kick, whether announced or unannounced) didn't surprise me. He was a tempo-setter. A player like that (makes) a big play, once a half, and everybody else picks up psychology-wise, on both sides of the ball."

Because the seemingly improvised kick was not mentioned the following day in a coaches' meeting back in California, Humenuik surmised that it possibly was something strictly between McKay and Rossovich.

Obbema, however, could not be convinced of that, based on what he had heard on the sideline right after the game ended.

Standing only about 10 feet away, Obbema overheard McKay chewing on Rossovich, something to the effect of "What the hell do you think you were doing?"

"I don't remember exactly what Tim said, but he looked at Coach McKay and basically said, 'It worked'," Obbema said. (The heroic effort by Rossovich – albeit not expected by the coaches – would be a follow-up to a key instance in which Rossovich had been involved earlier in the season opener against Washington State.) "Coach McKay called me over and asked me if I had anything to do with this onside kick. I said, 'Tim just said he was going to try and kick it right towards me, and I better catch it, or he was going to kick my ass.' "

As Obbema walked off the field shortly thereafter, he encountered a young fan, who snatched his helmet, not caring whether the sophomore was a star or reserve.

"There were tons of people, and I was just trying to get off the field, and he just grabbed it away from me. I wound up giving him my chin strap" as a souvenir, since the equipment manager back home would have not been happy if the helmet had disappeared without a valid explanation, Obbema said. "I mean, there were hundreds of people out on the field, and we were just trying to get out of there."

It took a long time to vacate the locker room because there were so many people waiting outside to greet the victors, who were dressed up in coats and ties. Those waiting included Obbema's great-aunt and other local family members who had ventured to South Bend from neighboring Illinois.

"It was a huge game – to beat them back there," 6-foot-1, 250-pound senior starting right guard Mike Scarpace said of the Fighting Irish. "It was the one team we had a hard time beating" for many years. Scarpace, now 66, earned a master's degree at USC, then taught physical education and coached mostly at the junior-college level in California for about four decades before going into semi-retirement at his current home near Thousand Oaks, Calif., northwest of Los Angeles, where he has helped coach at a nearby high school.

Even squad members who were injured and had to stay back in Southern California derived great joy from seeing the jinx snapped because the game was nationally televised. One of them was 240-pound reserve offensive lineman Jim Melillo, who, when healthy, backed up either starting tackle, Yary, and another future NFL player, Mike Taylor.

"It was a tremendous victory . . . the first after all those years" in South Bend, said Melillo, a San Diego area Trojan who was rehabilitating from a knee injury that would keep him out of action for the rest of the season. Melillo incurred the injury earlier in practice when hit sideways by a teammate who had recently been moved from running back to the offensive line and was over-eager in trying to demonstrate his prowess to the coaching staff.

There was a marked difference on the return flight compared to the trip to Notre Dame – one between nervousness and happiness. "We accomplished what we set out to do: Beat Notre Dame back there . . . tremendous satisfaction, but we knew we still had some tough games coming up. When you're No. 1 in the nation, everyone's gonna play their best game against you," Obbema said.

Legendary Green Bay coach Vince Lombardi used to describe football as 95 percent mental and 5 percent physical. "You think all you have to do is show up, but that's not true because these guys (opponents) want to win, too," regardless of whether that opponent is a decided underdog, Obbema said.

Many opposing players had wanted to play at USC, but were not recruited by the school, so those foes "wanted to show they were every bit as good." The result almost always was teams that faced the Trojans playing above their ability, trying things they normally would not do, such as trick plays.

Obbema was not unlike most of his college teammates, who were accustomed to winning at every level: His teams had a composite record of 83-7-2 in a span that included two years in Pop Warner, three years at Mater Dei and four years at USC.

Unofficial recruiting coordinator Dekeado (pronounced DUH-KAY-DOE) said he had at least one way to help calm Joe Obbema's pre-game nervousness.

"I wanted to give a plug to Bud Furillo about Joe Obbema before the Notre Dame game because Joe was nervous," Dekeado said. (The late Furillo was sports editor of the since-defunct *Los Angeles Herald-Examiner*. Furillo, who got his nickname, "the Steamer," from a regular column called "The Steam Room," died in 2006 at age 80.)

Despite the glee associated with a flight home after a huge win, a lot of the passengers on the charter were scratching their heads, wondering why the plane seemed to land prematurely, and take off again soon, rather than flying non-stop to Los Angeles. Actually, Obbema and others around him heard a story circulating around the cabin regarding the early landing not long after the plane had left Chicago – one which was never officially confirmed or denied.

"If I remember right, we landed in Omaha because the alumni ran out of refreshments," he said. "It was only a rumor, but who knows?" Considering what usually occurred in First Class, and because this was a charter flight, the rumors that abounded were probably true, and at least one other player suspected the same.

"That sounds a little familiar. The alumni were wild coming back," said Lehmer, who had ruined his neck while playing college football but endured and, with another Trojan-turned-orthopedic-surgeon, Fred Khasigian, was awarded an NCAA Postgraduate Scholarship in 1969 (teammate Steve Sogge had earned a similar award in 1968. Because of his USC injury, Lehmer underwent spine fusion surgery about 10 years ago; he since has had to forgo performing the 12-hour spine surgery that he had practiced for years, transforming into a consulting surgeon instead.)

A couple of hours later, the aircraft began going in circles, and when players, coaches and others looked out into the darkness, they could not clearly see the massive collection of city lights around Los Angeles – only many clouds.

"LAX (Los Angeles International Airport) was fogged in and closed, and we circled LAX for hours" on the victorious return flight, said 235-pound starting center Allmon, a longtime successful businessman in the City of Angels. "There were maybe 15,000 USC rooters filling the terminal and out into the street.

"Somehow, there was an 'immaculate moment,' and we were the only plane allowed to land. We honestly didn't know if it was God looking after us or (whether) John McKay had parted the clouds," said the 66-year-old Allmon.

"There were thousands of people, and everybody was crazy, screaming . . . It was beautiful," Lehmer said of the adoring airport throng.

Reflecting on their playing days together, Lehmer described Obbema as "a little bit wild," a description that Obbema himself will *never* deny. "But he was a good football player and a hard hitter; I liked him and respected him." The semi-retired surgeon said he and Obbema "knew each other well since we were in the same class and both were from

Orange County, and there weren't that many Orange County players" on the USC roster.

In the summer immediately preceding their eventually hooking up as teammates in Cardinal-and-Gold in 1966, the pair were opponents in the Orange County All-Star game on Obbema's old Mater Dei home turf, the Santa Ana Bowl, Obbema for the South, Lehmer the North. Lehmer enrolled at USC following a semester at Fullerton Junior College, in time to participate in 1967 spring practice at Troy. Although today living almost 2,000 miles from each other, the two stay in touch occasionally on the phone, still comparing notes on various injuries incurred on the gridiron many years previously.

2

SLOGGING THROUGH THE MUD

AND THE MUCK

Life is made up of marble and mud.

-- The House of the Seven Gables, 2, Nathaniel Hawthorne (1804-1864)

The Trojans had opened the 1967 season in decisive fashion, drubbing Washington State on the road, 49-0. They followed up the next week in a rare night game back home at the Coliseum by beating Texas, 17-13. Then ensued a 21-17 road victory at Michigan State and a 30-0 shutout of invading Stanford the week before traveling to Notre Dame to break the jinx.

After the clash with the Irish, USC rolled past three conference opponents: host Washington (23-6), visiting Oregon (28-6) and host California (31-

12). However, it was a maddening mire of muck at Oregon State that provided the season's only black mark exactly a week prior to clashing with UCLA.

Roughly two months before encountering the muddy field, though, the season would open at another northern venue – and it was on visits to those four Pacific Northwest conference opponents that often produced strange doings. For once, that did not happen on the rolling plains of eastern Washington, however. As he would do a month later at Notre Dame, big Tim Rossovich produced a game-changing moment on the first play in that decisive opener against the WSU Cougars in remote Palouse Country. His "little brother" and fellow defensive player Joe Obbema always wore customized socks and non-adhesive gauze since his skin was sensitive to normal, gauzy athletic tape that included adhesive material.

Against Washington State, as was the case on every game day, each of the Trojans was given a new pair of standard-issue wool socks, but this time Rossovich decided to separate the new pair in an unusual way.

"The thing about Tim pulling the socks apart was, he didn't pull them apart at the seams," Obbema said. "It was the most incredible thing I've ever seen. It's next to impossible (pulling the socks apart away from the seams). I tried it and couldn't do it, and I was a very strong boy at the time."

Washington State coach Jim Sweeney installed a Wishbone-type offense involving running the option without a block. USC Head Coach John McKay had diagrammed the exact play for Rossovich, Obbema and fellow defensive ends Jimmy Gunn and Bill Hayhoe on the blackboard during the week, so they were prepared for it.

"Coach McKay told us, 'They're gonna block you boys,' " Obbema said. Then when Rossovich asked what the coach meant by that, since the Wishbone, or triple option, typically didn't have offensive blockers aim at defensive ends or outside linebackers, McKay explained that he really wanted to encourage the opposing quarterback to be disrupted by pitching the ball too soon to a trailing back.

So in the game, the Cougars ran the initial play toward Rossovich, who broke the tailback's sternum with a sure tackle. Because WSU had no one else to run the Wishbone, the Cougars reverted to the I-formation for the duration.

Throughout his long college and pro careers, Rossovich was known as one of the game's hardest hitters but one who did the job in "clean" fashion.

"I learned how to play linebacker from (watching) Dick Butkus," the Chicago Bears' Hall of Fame middle backer, Rossovich said. "You put your forehead under their chin and make them snap back and make their legs go under, and send them back to the bench – go to the sidelines (to) get some smelling salts." "Rosso" said he *never* intended to end an opposing player's career or cause something like a serious knee injury; a clean hit to the sternum, however, was just another day at the "office."

Because USC was traditionally an I-formation team itself, its players were used to seeing that set daily in practice, in addition to the preparatory chalk sessions during the week, so the defensive players always adjusted well on a weekly basis. That familiarity made the adjustment almost foolproof.

"The system was built to where adjustments were easy to make," said assistant offensive line coach Rod Humenuik, who later was an assistant in the National Football League for years and also head coach of a since-defunct college program at California State-Northridge. "It was like a ladder, from the bottom rung on up. Then the next rung up was the situation."

With the system already firmly in place, each situation then was considered. And with the '67

USC squad being upper-class-heavy (with only nine sophomores, including Obbema), the adjustments occurred with relative ease.

The Trojans looked to recruit players to fit the system. Humenuik said it helped having mostly intelligent, adaptable individuals, who happened to be among the nation's most-gifted players.

He said the atmosphere – and relationship between players – always has been different in the pros and college ranks, and that it changed even more over the 40-plus years he coached.

"I would tell the college players, 'My job is to make you better.' In the NFL, you would tell them, 'I wanna make you better so you can make more money'," Humenuik said. At either level, as he further put it, "Praise will raise."

Junior center Dick Allmon, a product of the upscale San Diego suburb of La Jolla who has since gone on to start several successful businesses from scratch, was one of those players Humenuik had in mind.

"There were so many good people . . . that the difference between playing and not playing" for the Trojans "was an eyelash," Allmon said.

"We had a very intelligent offensive line – if you consider I'm the only guy without an advanced degree," he said, nonetheless adding that he *did* earn a bachelor's degree in Business. That level of consummate intelligence allowed a lot of adapting on the field. At least two of those who played on the interior line during Allmon's time at USC, Steve Lehmer and Fred Khasigian, eventually became orthopedic surgeons practicing only 25 miles apart in Northern California.

Veteran USC radio play-by-play man Tom Kelly, now in his mid-80s and living in Encino, Calif., carried Allmon's comments a step further. Kelly said the 1967 team "all played so well" because the starters always had somebody equally as good pushing them from behind on "an amazing football team of stars." Amid all this enormous talent, Kelly said of someone like Obbema, "he was almost the forgotten man."

Following the win over Texas, in which Obbema broke his left ring finger on the opening kickoff but the team trainer was somehow able to pop it back into place, Obbema was able to resume playing.

"He looked at me and told me, 'You broke your finger' and I said, 'I know.'" That preceded the tight escape at Michigan State; then it was time for the opponent many Trojan players savored to face.

As much pleasure as USC players had in winning rivalry games like UCLA and Notre Dame, they really wanted to beat Stanford more than anybody else. The Cardinal (then still known as the Indians until political correctness forced a mascot change) had always fashioned themselves as a Western version of Ivy Leaguers, considering themselves intellectually superior to the other conference schools.

The irony in that thought process for someone like Obbema was that, probably like a lot of his brainy teammates, he had scored 1,300-plus on the Scholastic Aptitude Tests and had his choice of colleges, including Stanford, before opting for Southern Cal. In fact, that score was good enough that he could have gone to Yale or other Ivy League schools.

In the back-to-back wins over Oregon and California, O.J. Simpson was sidelined with a rib injury, but was aptly spelled by 6-foot, 205-pound senior backup Steve Grady. Grady had been a highly touted High School All-American at Loyola High School, not far from the USC campus; he eventually coached for 30 years at his prep alma mater, most as head coach, before retiring to continue as a counselor at Loyola. He is the only one in California prep history to be both player of the year (1962) and coach of the year (2003).

"I was the clean-up detail," Grady said, all too modestly. Entering the game against the invading Ducks in the second quarter, he piled up more than 100 rushing yards. He repeated the century feat the following week at Cal, playing the entire game at tailback. (In high school, Grady had been the last of a breed – a single-wing tailback who always took a direct snap from center, not unlike today's shotgun or "Wildcat" formations. His Loyola team built a then-record 35-game win streak against some of California's toughest big-school competition.)

Grady was heavily recruited by many schools but chose the Trojans, not being able to predict that one of the greatest running backs of all time, Simpson,whose teammates were the first to call him The Juice, would later transfer from a junior college in San Francisco to eclipse the talented Grady for the starting job.

"There were a number of things. The cream of the crop gets recruited. Timing wasn't the best, with O.J. also there," Grady said of a sometimes-bittersweet college playing career in Troy.

Grady's talent and proven numbers when spelling Simpson against optimum competition prompted a teammate to dub Grady "the best running back no one ever heard of."

While there generally was overall harmony (after all, this was a team competing every year, it seemed, for a national championship), all was not necessarily perfect, as junior reserve offensive lineman Jim Melillo put it.

He described his existence as somewhat of a nightmare after he had transferred from a junior college, Southwestern, near San Diego, even having eagerly reported to USC early to participate in spring drills. The 6-foot-3, 240-pound Melillo was initially recruited to play defense, but eventually was switched to offense.

"I wasn't in that inner circle . . . when they jerked my string," he said. "I was kind of on the outside looking in. In every program, there's a clique." But he nevertheless was grateful for having the opportunity to compete, not just in 1967 yet also 1968, for the national title. Like Obbema, Melillo saw a lot of special-teams action, and was impressed by his tenacious, slightly younger teammate.

"Joe was a tough, hard-nosed guy, a tough cookie despite not playing much," the San Diegan said. "We had lots of tremendous athletes, like Rossovich and other tremendous physical specimens," which was commonplace in most successful major-college programs. That was a time before the National Collegiate Athletic Association set limits on the number of athletic scholarships, so there were more scholarship players than is currently the case. "Joe wasn't one of those (specimens), but he could really rock you," said Melillo, also a more-than-capable baseball catcher who flirted with the idea of playing for USC's often-top-rated squad in that sport.

The late backup defensive lineman Doug Mooers, an Air Force transfer, said he thought favoritism existed among the coaching staff. Never satisfied at USC despite being on the roster of a national champion and Rose Bowl winner, Mooers transferred again between his junior and senior years to Whittier College, a small National Association of Intercollegiate Athletics school about 15 miles away. Because the Whittier Poets were not an NCAA member, he could play immediately. However, due to a torn hamstring, at Whittier, he never practiced during the week but played every Saturday at the alma mater of the late President Richard Nixon.

An interesting postscript from Mooers despite his having left the Trojan program: The players on that USC team, regardless of whether they started, were good enough to have been first-stringers at most any other major college. Moreover, Mooers said, not long before dying of cancer in 2011, they likely could have been able to beat a lower-level pro team such as the original incarnation of the New Orleans Saints for whom he later played. The old Saints, known widely as the "Ain'ts," were so bad that their fans covered their heads with paper bags.

For his part, Humenuik had little daily interaction with Obbema, Mooers and the other defensive players. But like his colleagues, the assistant offensive line coach shared locker-room camaraderie with players, whereby an offensive coach would occasionally offer his firsthand expertise and counsel to the defenders. Because of that mutual relationship, coach and player developed further kinship, which allowed honest evaluations generally to flow like a calming stream.

"He had an excellent work ethic," Humenuik said of Obbema. "He was a joy to coach because he was open-minded – in the sense that he was able to listen" and adjust just like the more-seasoned teammates. "Joe had good size, plus in the locker room, he just got along well with everybody. Those

were things Dick Coury had mentioned about him"
when Obbema first got to USC after his entire prep
career at Mater Dei under Coury.

When the Trojans ultimately traveled north to
Corvallis to face the host Oregon State Beavers, it
was after a couple of days of monsoon downpours
on a field that never was in good condition even
when it was not raining. Furthermore, the grounds
crew apparently had unveiled some handy hoses
before the game.

The field conditions received reviews –
mostly negative -- from some of the Trojans. The
playing surface had not been covered in three days,
which was not something apparently foreign to the
Beavers' tricky head coach, the late Dee Andros.
He had earned the moniker "The Great Pumpkin"
because he was a fairly large, round man, and
because one of OSU's primary colors was orange,
he often wore a sport coat of that color. (Some wags
have speculated that Andros liked the field to be
wet, so as to be able to grow Beaver-orange
pumpkins there after the season ended.)

"It was terrible weather and the field was a
mess," broadcaster Kelly said. He said it effectively

made it "a level playing field," which bad weather tends to do in an otherwise-uneven matchup.

For Obbema, the conditions harkened back mentally to his Pop Warner days as an 11- and 12-year-old back in Buena Park. "We were playing in the Berry Bowl . . . and it poured and poured and poured," he said.

Tackle Ron Yary, voted the nation's top interior lineman and awarded the Outland Trophy at season's end, said during his playing career – from high school through college to the pros – he never worried about the field or weather conditions. "It's not relevant . . . It's just an excuse," he said. "You can pick a lot of other reasons why you lose."

Coach Humenuik concurred – at least to a degree – saying, "You gotta be prepared to play under any conditions. There were no artificial turf or domes" back then.

That day, USC players changed cleats and did everything possible to counteract the speed being neutralized by the muddy ground. When players put their feet down, it was done carefully on the choppy turf. Humenuik compared weather preparations to a few years down the road as a New England Patriots' assistant when the team would go into mile-high

Denver early to acclimate to the rarefied air rather than field conditions.

In that era, before fake "grass" and domed stadiums became more commonplace, Grady said a muddy grass field like in the Beavers' stadium that afternoon was simply slippery, so he had to be careful as he blocked, in spelling Simpson on certain plays, when reserve fullback Mike Hull carried the ball.

"It was terrible," weak-side (left) guard Lehmer conceded, likening the OSU field to a "pigsty," and terming it a "mud pit." (Lehmer was the weak-side guard any time one of the big tight ends, Bob Klein or Bob Miller, set up on the right, or strong, side.) Lehmer said it reminded him of "sandlot football in a storm. I was stepping into big mud holes, I was slipping, and there was no traction."

Tall defensive lineman Hayhoe, standing 6-foot-8, later played seven seasons as an offensive tackle with the Green Bay Packers. Therefore, he would spend many future wintry Wisconsin afternoons battling elements much more brutal than those in Corvallis.

"It was pretty muddy, and the grass was real long" on the Beavers' field, said Hayhoe, who has lived in Sparks, Nev., outside Reno, for many years since retiring from the Packers. "I guess it worked; it slowed O.J. down.

"I sort of enjoyed playing in different types of weather," he said. (Hayhoe, who is now 66 years old, also said that in his NFL playing days, Green Bay had no indoor practice field, so when the Packers went indoors for drills, they did it in a local hotel's convention center. Also during that time, it was before ex-college teammate Yary and the archrival Minnesota Vikings had moved into their Metrodome (now Mall of America Field).

Therefore, when playing outdoors at old Metropolitan Stadium, Hayhoe said "it felt like concrete or pavement. They used to warm the field with flame-throwers."

Apparently, Hayhoe paid the price for competing all those years on either muddy or concrete-hard surfaces as a Packer because he broke his right leg three times, once so badly that he missed an entire season. The result has been two ankle fusions, the most recent in 2009, leaving him with an ankle that never has healed.

Another Trojan, who also lined up alongside Hayhoe at Birmingham High School in the San Fernando Valley, was philosophical about the '67

Oregon State game but lent a different twist from anyone else – at least publicly. There is nothing he can do about it now – more than four decades after the fact – but offensive strong-side (right) guard Mike Scarpace said that, from where he stood on the sidelines in Corvallis, the third-period, 30-yard field goal by Mike Haggard that "won" the game for Oregon State "wasn't good; it was way off to the left."

"I remember the guys getting upset about it," said Lehmer, who added that he could not say whether the deciding kick had missed or not despite standing next to Scarpace between offensive rotations.

Obbema was on the field on the kick-blocking unit when the ostensibly winning field goal was booted. He dove to try and block the kick but missed. So after it cleared the line of scrimmage, he automatically turned to watch the ball's flight.

"I looked at the back judge, and he already had his hands up" to signify a successful attempt "even before it cleared the crossbar," Obbema said.

Dick "Litz" Litzinger, who had preceded Obbema as Mater Dei's star linebacker before playing on a Junior Rose Bowl-winning Santa Ana

College squad, wound up at the University of Idaho, Andros's last previous head-coaching stop.

Litz, now in his late 60s, admitted that, before the Idaho Vandals constructed their snazzy, new Kibbie Dome indoor facility, Andros, who died in 2003, was known to order, for their rare home games, a pre-game soaking of the natural-grass-and-dirt surface on the old, 1930s-vintage field. According to GoVandals.com, the school's official athletic website, the old stadium burned down in 1969, probably in a fire set by some opponent that did not want to play in the mud anymore.

"We played most of our games away because we needed the money," Litz said of the big guarantees visiting schools received at such storied locales as Missouri or Utah. "We all loved to play for Dee," he said of the Idaho group that had 15 players drafted into the pros – NFL, AFL or Canadian league -- in 1965 alone. (Let it be said, then, with such an exemplary track record, that, unlike the field, Andros' own players were *not* "watered down.")

Litz also compared the defensive situation of 40-plus years ago to today's scenario. "I think it's like (Baltimore's) Ray Lewis . . . when you're a linebacker, especially a middle linebacker, you're in on every play. You zero in on the opponent on pursuit and make that alley right in the hole," he said. Like himself, he noted, Obbema was precisely that type of player, leading the defense by tacit example with a contagious individual intensity.

Back in Corvallis in '67, meanwhile, Joe Obbema had a good spot on the sideline to watch star tailback Simpson try to dart and dance – and splash – through initial holes when the USC offense had the ball, almost breaking loose for what would have been the deciding touchdown. Trouble was, the game's only score in the muck and mire was on that aforementioned second-half field goal by the underdog Beavers. And, if you believe Scarpace and Obbema, even *that* was not legitimate.

"We ran a play called 27-pitch, which was a play for O.J. to go around the corners. I was on the sidelines about 10 yards away from the defensive back who came up to tackle him," Obbema said. "He did everything right; he got on balance and, as the defensive back attempted to tackle O.J., he missed him and came up with a full face of mud."

Obbema caught eye contact with the OSU defender, who wore an expression that could have easily translated to "I thought I did everything right, but *what* did I do wrong?"

Obbema's older teammate, Scarpace, looks back on that specific play with perhaps an unnecessary bit of personal contrition.

"I was the pulling guard on that play with O.J., who was caught from behind," Scarpace said. "When I fell down, I should've turned around to block the guy ahead of him. The mud was up to our calves that day.

"Now they coach going to the outside to avoid the middle of the field," which is churned up on each play by the constant motion of legs pushing cleated soles into the dirt or mud, Scarpace added.

(The author requested permission from the Nevada Department of Corrections to interview O.J. Simpson, but the request was denied. A spokeswoman for the department said Simpson is regarded as a "high-profile" inmate and, therefore, is not available for interviews. Simpson is serving at least a nine-year sentence at the Lovelock Correctional Center in northern Nevada for armed robbery, kidnapping and other felonies. Simpson was found guilty in 2008 in conjunction with a 2007 raid on a memorabilia collector's Las Vegas home to recover what the longtime running back and broadcaster felt were items belonging to him. He filed a motion for a new trial in May 2013 because of alleged lawyer malfeasance, but the motion was denied. Most former USC teammates of Simpson who were interviewed for this book concede that his current incarnation is "a different person" from the speedy, happy-go-lucky guy they knew and played with back in the late '60s.)

(Coincidentally, Joe Obbema's stepson, Nathan Kennett, was a correctional officer at Nevada's Indian Springs facility, readying for a permanent move back to Texas, when Simpson was first incarcerated at Indian Springs before being quickly transferred north to Lovelock, but had no personal contact with "Inmate Simpson.")

Other than the muddy field conditions at Corvallis, Obbema and Co. were facing a player whom he considered to be his toughest individual opponent in both 1967 and 1968, the OSU fullback, Bill Enyart, who was known as "Earthquake." He was called that because opposing players swore that they could hear the ground rumble under him, wet conditions notwithstanding, anytime the muscular workhorse bulldozed his way forward. (Enyart was listed at 235 pounds, but some Trojans – and others – believed he ran closer to 270 or 275.)

"He had calves like tree stumps, like a big farm boy," Mooers said of Enyart. "They were physically imposing, a very large team," Allmon said of the Beavers. "But we were so much faster.

How do you slow down speed?" He asked rhetorically before quickly answering his own question, "You wet the field."

Allmon said one of his teammates, who had played in high school with an Oregon State counterpart, confided that the Beaver had told him about Andros watering the field. "It was so thick, you could hardly move in it," the USC center said.

Humenuik said he thought Enyart may have set a single-game record for carries that afternoon because the huge pile-driver seemed to tote the ball on every down. "They ran constant dives with him – right, left," he said. Enyart rolled up 135 rushing yards.

While the eventual 1967 Heisman Trophy winner, UCLA quarterback Gary Beban, was better-publicized, Obbema and many of his teammates felt Enyart was the best individual they faced all season.

An example was another play in the mud game. The Trojans double-teamed the tackle and end with Obbema and defensive tackle Al Cowlings, something for which they had prepared all week. Obbema and Cowlings lined up on the wingback, isolated on either of the Beavers' "Bam-Bam" halfbacks, Bob Mayes or Bill Main. Even though there was the double-team, and Enyart seemed thwarted by hard hits, he nonetheless bulled ahead for gain after gain. Such a play was the rule, not the exception, with Earthquake Enyart.

Before Obbema left the field at game's end, Enyart stopped him, and the huge fullback asked, "What the hell did you hit me with?" And the exasperated Obbema told him, "Everything I had."

Tim Rossovich thought it was ironic that, despite being voted consensus national champions by season's end, the Trojans should have the 3-0 loss as their one major negative, especially since USC only allowed a total of only 87 points in 1967.

He also retrospectively second-guessed that day's strategy by his coaches.

"You know what John McKay should've done? Put O.J. on the bench and put Grady in the game," he said. "We were ankle-deep in mud. Enyart weighed more than 50 pounds more than anybody on our defensive line. Nobody could stand up" to set up for the type of "clean" tackle that was his trademark, Rossovich said.

The end result that day, amid the off-and-on rain, was the Trojans dropping to No. 2 in the nation.

He didn't realize it then but, like Hayhoe and Yary, Rossovich, would encounter sometimes even more-adverse weather playing in the NFL – despite being based in sunny San Diego on the downswing of his pro career. The Chargers, after all, competed annually in their division in occasional winter wonderlands like Denver and Kansas City. Rossovich's first pro stop had been in another city known for an unpredictable climate, Philadelphia.

Predictably, Rossovich admitted that "the coldest game I ever played in was in Denver. The field was like an ice rink," he said, reminiscing about the same locale as did Humenuik but not using the typical altitude complaint regarding Colorado's capital city. Rossovich said one of his star teammates, Louisiana-bred wide receiver Gary Garrison, who played collegiately at warm-weather San Diego State, had been ejected from that game in the early '70s for removing the cleats from his shoes, using the resultant flatter soles to gain added traction – a no-no in the heavily regulated NFL, even back then.

As the fates also would eventually have it, Earthquake and The Juice wound up as pro teammates for two years, 1969-70, in a place, not unlike Green Bay, with football weather usually

much worse than Corvallis, or Denver, or Kansas
City: Buffalo, N.Y.

3

BLOOMING WITH THE ROSES

It was roses, roses all the way.

-- The Patriot (1845), st. 1, Robert Browning (1812-1889)

Aspirations of regaining the national No.1 after the final regular season game in 1967 "gave us a ray of hope," Joe Obbema said. "It's never easy to prepare after a loss," but that hopeful attitude "made us practice as hard as we could."

USC players and coaches knew they had to beat crosstown archrival UCLA to win the national championship because they realized the two polling entities – college coaches nationwide in one case, and sportswriters in the other -- voted after the last game.

Even though the Bruins had admittedly outplayed the Trojans most of the game, it was a critical, third-and-8 pass play with another former Mater Dei star, senior Toby Page, at quarterback. The 6-foot Page shared quarterbacking duties all season with shorter (5-foot-10) but sure-armed Steve Sogge, who had started yet left early in the contest. (A third quarterback on the USC roster in the '67 season was 6-foot-4 San Franciscan Mike Holmgren. A sophomore like Obbema, he would go on to coach the Green Bay Packers to the 1998 Super Bowl title, then enjoy a long tenure as the Seattle Seahawks' head man before being hired as the Cleveland Browns' team president after the regular season ended in 2009. He left the Browns in 2012 following an ownership change.)

A certain inside and firsthand recounting of the situation on one of the most famous plays in college football history has not been told for public consumption until now – at least from the offensive linemen's perspective, and that of their teammates watching anxiously on the sideline. In fact, with a small twist or turn, the play, and final result, might never have turned out as successfully as it did.

"The hot color was red. Toby called red-23 (or 23-blast). Steve Lehmer (a sophomore guard from Anaheim's Loara High School, not far from

Mater Dei), is extremely intelligent and is a doctor now . . . and he didn't hear it. So he pass-blocked for a split-second, and Don Manning of UCLA backpedaled a bit, thinking pass, and (O.J.) Simpson took the handoff and scored the winning touchdown," Obbema said. Rikki Aldridge, like Obbema and Lehmer a fellow Orange County product, from Westminster, then booted the deciding point-after to enable the voters in both polls to boost the Trojans back into the final No. 1 slot when the regular season concluded.

"That was the most memorable single play in my college career, and a screw-up that turned into a blessing," Lehmer hinted, offering a glance at the psychiatry profession that he almost pursued before settling on becoming an orthopedic surgeon. "I would've been a major horse's ass. . . . I think that was the only play I blew in a game that year."

Because a pass play was called, Lehmer automatically set up in a pass-blocking stance, with less weight forward, causing Manning, the All-America linebacker who was reading him, to back into a zone. In a split-second, after the momentary distraction, however, Lehmer quickly detected the audible and started to go forward. Actually, each lineman had adjusted when the audible was called.

The Trojans' highly intelligent offensive linemen were accustomed anyway to doing a lot of trap-blocking, enabling Simpson and other USC runners to get loose often on counter plays like red-23.

After Lehmer's adjustment, he said, "O.J. came behind me, forcing him to the left. It was serendipitous," the articulate sophomore guard said. "Then I watched the rest of the way as O.J. kept going downfield. I was very thankful, and pissed off. I said to (line coach Dave) Levy, 'I blew the play, I blew the play,' and he said, 'It doesn't matter'."

Page said he called the audible himself when he saw Manning move; he said check-offs rarely came from the bench.

When the ball was snapped, Simpson recalled in the 2004 book, *The Heisman*, by Bill Pennington, "it was all instinct."

In a revealing disclosure that it seems also did not surface until now in belated recollections, the spectacular play almost *never* happened from another standpoint, according to junior center Dick Allmon, who experienced similar schizoid-like feelings to those of his younger "acolyte" Lehmer.

"I almost knocked him down twice," Allmon said of Simpson. "On the left side, I got free and headed for the (outside linebacker) on that side and, in doing so, I knocked O.J. to the outside."

Then, Allmon said he and Simpson physically intersected again as Allmon sprinted straight ahead as quickly as a 235-pound lineman could, and the Heisman Trophy candidate cut a right angle before racing downfield for the score. The whole game, the savvy center said, the opposing Bruins "tried to take the outside play away from O.J. on the pitch play. UCLA used an extra-wide defense; they left the middle open by spreading the tackles," he said.

From the sideline, as Steve Grady readied himself for any play when Simpson might go down and thrust him back into the game, instead the backup tailback watched in awe with the rest of the team.

"It's just that we were behind . . . I didn't know it was an audible (play change) at the time," Grady said. "He cut back toward our sideline. You can see in the pictures how we're all jumping up and down."

The audible and resultant adjustment occurred because the Bruins were overplaying the

Trojan offense, even though UCLA had largely outplayed their archrivals in the first half.

"But they kept running the ball when they should've passed more. We kept on stopping them, and (Gary) Beban had injured his ribs," the other starting guard, senior Mike Scarpace, said of the UCLA senior quarterback who won that year's Heisman Trophy, edging out Simpson, who earned the award the next season.

Improvisation that happened within the USC interior line was a frequent occurrence. For instance, Lehmer would do a lot of cross-blocking with left tackle Taylor. That was interesting in retrospect since the two wound up living just a few miles from each other outside Sacramento, Calif., after Taylor completed an NFL career and opened a barbecue restaurant in nearby Folsom.

The adjustments by the cerebral offensive linemen did not go unnoticed by at least one key defensive star.

"I appreciated their ability to work as a unit and help each other out, and adjust. They were very cohesive," All-America end/outside linebacker Tim Rossovich said of the linemen he faced each day in practice. Rossovich, an extremely disciplined operative on the field but a widely known "crazy man" off the field, said the big blockers, who were like a well-oiled machine, contrasted greatly with defenders like himself who he said were "a lot of renegades."

(For the record, while USC was doing "surgery" on most '67 opponents, Lehmer and two other members of that squad, also from the same city, rover Ty Salness from Anaheim High, and linebacker Bob Jensen from Magnolia, eventually became doctors or dentists. A fourth USC championship player, Fred Khasigian, became an orthopedic surgeon in Northern California, as did Lehmer. Salness wound up practicing geriatric and internal medicine in Idaho. Jensen is a retired dentist who figured in a later post-college episode involving Joe Obbema.)

Allmon said he and his fellow offensive linemen had *carte blanche* to improvise since the coaching staff could exploit the extreme collective intelligence of that tackle-to-tackle group, along with a pair of tall and talented tight ends in Bob Klein and Bob Miller, both 6-foot-5 and 230 pounds-plus.

"I put in a play called 'Banjo,' and Sogge ran a quarterback sneak for 15yards" in another game,

Allmon said. "It was something we could do because of the intelligence and adaptability" of the offensive front wall.

Six-foot-8, 265-pound Bill Hayhoe USC's "living, breathing giant," as someone once described him, and who had played with Scarpace at Birmingham High in the San Fernando Valley, blocked a field goal and point-after attempt against UCLA. That, coupled with a blocked extra-point try by Long Beach-reared teammate Tony Terry, proved the difference in the 21-20 Southern Cal win.

"I usually played on the outside" on opponents' kick attempts, Hayhoe said. But Head Coach John McKay positioned him on the inside for the UCLA game, primarily because McKay noticed that Zenon Andrusyshyn, the Bruins' German-born kicker of Ukrainian descent, had a low trajectory on his soccer-style kicks.

In most cases, all Hayhoe had to do, with his superior height, was stand straight up, then jump in the air with his arms extended upward. (While Hayhoe and Scarpace were at Birmingham, two classmates who were cheerleaders were Oscar-winning actress Sally Field and controversial financier-turned-philanthropist Michael Milken.)

76

Obbema conceded, as he told a *Los Angeles Times* columnist after the game, that it was the greatest game he's ever played in "because of all the implications – O.J. possibly winning the Heisman, 1 vs. 2, etcetera."

He said that "in all my time playing in the Coliseum, that, and the end of the game, was the first time I heard the home crowd" in the cavernous, bowl-shaped arena used in 1932 for the Olympic Games with a running track ringing the football field and able to accommodate more than 100,000 fans. (The huge, aging stadium still sits directly across Exposition Boulevard from USC, a 301-acre campus of mostly Romanesque-style buildings, with newer structures bearing what one might accurately term "*faux*-Romanesque" architecture.)

"Every time they show film of that game, they show No. 90 jumping up and down," Obbema said, echoing the excitement Grady had articulated.

Ironically, in addition to the feeling that crested for the national title run, the '67 Trojans embodied an island of racial harmony amid the turmoil that had happened only two years before just a few mere miles south straight down Vermont Avenue or the parallel Harbor Freeway in Watts. In fact, Obbema and fellow teammates always marveled at how well the black and white players on that team got along as if they were part of a tightly knit family with a common goal – one achieved by sewing up the national title on that warm November day.

"What stands out, first, our players, as a whole, played as one – a group of guys playing as one," Humenuik said, with a bit of marvel in his voice.

Any joy and tranquility in University Park, however, was not duplicated across town in Westwood. "It really took a toll on some of the UCLA guys – long-term mental and emotional implications," Obbema said of the one-point game, adding that "it was just the reverse for USC – a berserk locker room. Plus we get that ring that few people in the whole world have.

"The accolades we got after the game were incredible except for Beban getting the Heisman instead of O.J. But winning the Heisman Trophy is a process – it takes two or three years" (unless you're Johnny Manziel, maybe). It should be remembered that Simpson was in his first season at USC after transferring from City College of San Francisco, then won the Heisman in his second Trojan season.

In later years, Obbema said that, while working in the trucking business, he encountered one of his UCLA rivals from that day, Vic Lepisto.

"He told me he couldn't forget about it. He went over and tooled around Europe for a couple of years trying to forget about that game; it just tore him up. I'm sure that was the case with a lot of guys," Obbema said. "To lose the national championship by one point . . . is almost impossible to get over. It's better to lose by 30 points than to lose by one point."

Obbema reasoned that only something like table tennis or volleyball may be among the few sports where the winning team has to outscore the loser by at least two points – in football, of course, a single point is enough.

"It was devastating to them (the Bruins). We broke their backs, and broke their hearts," Lehmer said.

Speaking of Lehmer, the day after the big win, McKay gathered the defense in the film room to look at offensive-line films, and he kept running and re-running – backward and forward – the almost-aborted red-23 play. All along as he ran the reels, McKay kept repeating, "We won the 1967 national championship on a sophomore mistake."

Obbema said he remembers assistant coach Levy reminding the team: "You're going to be getting a ring in about a month. Getting this ring would be a big thing. He was dead right." However, Obbema said that, as he ages, "in the past 10-15 years, it has meant more." He said that in all his years in business, people always noticed he had played for the USC national champions simply by seeing that ring. "It's like the Super Bowl ring of college; not many people have one."

When the championship rings finally were delivered by the company that designed them, a funny thing happened. The rings were engraved on the inside with each player or coach's initials or name -- the first name and last name for most of the players.

"It turned out they handed me O.J.'s ring and I tried it on and it didn't exactly fit my hand, of course, and I thought, wait a minute, this isn't my ring, and gave it back to him – but maybe I should've kept that ring; J.O., O.J. Honest mistake," Obbema said.

It was easy to exchange for the proper rings, though, since Simpson and Obbema had been stall mates the entire '68 season; McKay had tried the former Mater Dei star at fullback, but the latter admitted, "I wasn't quick enough to lead for O.J., so

I went back on defense and special teams." During the trial at fullback, Obbema wore uniform No. 34 (Simpson was No. 32). Obbema's stall mate in both '67 & the one game he in which he played in '69 was Jimmy Gunn, the star defensive end and linebacker out of San Diego; Obbema was No. 90 those two years.

The correct-fitting piece of gold jewelry encased with a cardinal stone that has been on Obbema's right ring finger since that day has a particular significance in the rest of Joe Obbema's bittersweet story. In fact, had he followed doctor's orders back in eighth grade, Obbema never would have played a down of football again.

That 1967 season as consensus national champions was punctuated on New Year's Day 1968 with a 14-3 Rose Bowl win over the Big Ten titlist Indiana Hoosiers, coached by Johnny Pont. USC finished with a 10-1 record; the only blemish lay back there in the mud and muck of Corvallis, Ore. Just a few months after the bowl triumph, Yary, who lined up in practice daily across from Obbema and Co. and who had added the Walter Camp Award as American football Player of the Year to the Outland honor, went first overall in the NFL draft.

It was all in marked contrast to that season's beginning.

Obbema said McKay had walked in to an early team meeting after the first practice that season and pronounced, "The 1967 Trojan football team – and he screamed it – is out of fucking shape. He was mad, and I was so glad I was in shape; God Almighty, he ran us to death." He said the legendary head coach whispered a knowing aside to Obbema to acknowledge the sophomore's superior conditioning, which was a testament to his own self-discipline coupled with coach Dick Coury's strong work attitude with his players at Mater Dei.

"He had us running repeat 40s, and guys were throwing up, falling down, quitting . . . but we were in shape by the time the two-a-days were over" – as evidenced "on the flesh" by season's end with the championship rings affixed to each player's and coach's fingers.

Allmon, who also started at center in 1968, his senior year, did not offer his name in the NFL draft, and, like Joe Obbema, never played organized football again. But the businessman-to-be said he not only did not regret it; he also was hardly disappointed a quarter-century later when Los Angeles lost its last NFL franchises, as the NFC

Rams bolted to St. Louis and the AFC Raiders returned to Oakland.

"Actually, I like it from a personal standpoint," Allmon said. "Playing in this town, there's real recognition. I think it enhances the Trojan scene . . . because I like college football an immense amount." Allmon added that the USC-UCLA rivalry is big enough to stand on its own, pro football in the city or not.

He also said there is one aspect of college – and pro – football he abhors: The increasing presence of "brutal" drugs and substance abuse, with steroids, and other artificial performance-enhancers and non-useful narcotics.

"The physics of the game have changed. They hit each other, and they're twice as big and twice as fast," said Allmon who spends each week running his business near downtown Los Angeles but flees on weekends to his home high above the smog in the thinner alpine air of the San Bernardino Mountains at Lake Arrowhead.

4

FUNNY YOU SHOULD ASK, COACH

Everything is funny as long as it is happening to somebody else.

-- The Illiterate Digest, P. 152, Will(iam Penn Adair) Rogers (1879-1935)

The 1968 season – Joe Obbema's junior year and one in which he started seven games on defense, mostly as a linebacker-like, stand-up end – was somewhat anti-climactic with the Trojans finishing at 9-1-1, and winning the Pac-8 title again, but blowing an early 10-0 lead and losing, 27-16, to Big Ten titlist Ohio State, coached by Woody Hayes, in the 1969 Rose Bowl. USC beat all comers in the regular season except Notre Dame, which tied the Trojans, 21-21, in the LA Coliseum.

Obbema remembers that Hayes's defensive backfield coach in that bowl contest was Lou Holtz, now a colorful analyst for the ESPN sports network who went on to be head coach for six different major-college football programs along with a short stint as head coach of the NFL's New York Jets.

Like John McKay, Holtz has been known for years as a naturally funny man who punctuated his humor with an extraordinarily quick wit.

Obbema relates the Mutt-and-Jeff tale of razor-thin Holtz racing down the sideline, trailed by the portly Hayes, as O.J. Simpson sprinted for a touchdown: "Coach Hayes asked Holtz how he could let him go 50 yards, and Holtz said he didn't go 55." Obbema had heard the incident recounted at a football clinic, but Holtz also included it in one of his autobiographical books, *Winning Every Day: The Game Plan for Success*.

"I'll tell you a story I heard about Lou Holtz that he tells at a clinic," the former USC player said. "He's talking about the inspiration and the things you can get out of your body and your mind, and how tough you can be, no matter what your status in life, and no matter big or strong or small, or whatever you are."

Obbema, still quoting Holtz, said, "I went down to the beach with my wife. She stood up and said, 'My, God, Lou, you're skinny.' And I looked at her and said, 'I'd like to point out that my lack of proficiency in my body prevented me from getting a better-looking wife, too.'"

As Obbema would agree, Lou Holtz is just a good, decent person; what you see on TV is what you get, and like John McKay, he is one of the most innately humorous head football coaches ever.

The difference between Holtz and the late McKay, Obbema said, was that the latter had a dry, sarcastic wit, while Holtz is simply funny, for whatever reason. Coincidentally, both coaches were born in the same state, West Virginia, plus both were devout Catholics.

Obbema used the 51-0 drubbing the Irish laid on USC in 1966 as an example of how McKay naturally injected gallows humor into many of his comments.

Said McKay at the time, responding to a reporter's question about what consolation he could find in the shutout loss: "The only solace I can take out of this game is that there are 700 million Chinese who don't know that SC played Notre Dame today." Obbema remembers that McKay told someone that, within the next several weeks, he received letters from correspondents in China.

Coaches were not the only funny fellows, whether any humor was intentional or not. Unexpected things happened during practice to break the ice, often involving the passionate assistant coach Marv Goux and an undersized backup linebacker named Reg Fielder, who, like Tim Rossovich, also fell into veteran assistant coach Dave Levy's category as a "self-appointed character."

In one instance, the team was in a room being exhorted with one of Goux's fiery "sermons" when Fielder innocently raised his hand in the back of the room and, whatever he asked, basically punctured Goux's "balloon."

Then one time during another practice, Phil Krueger, the defensive coordinator, summoned Fielder.

"Get over here," Krueger demanded, to which the 202-pounder didn't budge an inch. "I said get over here," Krueger insisted, raising his voice a few decibels, and Fielder replied, "I only answer to 'dirty little asshole.' Then Krueger replied back, "Then get over here, you dirty little asshole." At which point Fielder hustled over to the coach's side.

(Krueger had been head coach at then-Fresno State College for two seasons before signing on with McKay and Co., then after USC, was head coach at Utah State and later joined McKay on the Tampa Bay staff.)

Obbema tried hard but unsuccessfully to be Simpson's fullback in the first three games of '68, saying, "I was fast but not quick enough. I couldn't get off the ball quick enough."

While waiting for his next practice turn one day, Obbema had his arms extended in cross-wise fashion, and McKay shooed him off the field. Then when Obbema ran back on for the next set, the coach kicked him off twice more for a total of three consecutive times. After which, McKay told the would-be fullback, "Obbema, if you cross your arms like you don't care, I'm gonna send you back to Mater Dei in a pine box." In the coach's opinion, crossing one's arms thusly was a psychological connotation of apathy, or that one did not care.

One thing folks will tell you about Joe Obbema, however, and that is he *never* could be truly regarded as apathetic, even though he appeared that way one day to his fabled head coach. So it was not long before he was back happily, and starting often, at defensive end, telling himself: Do not cock your arms like that ever again.

When Obbema was a freshman, the yearlings were not allowed to play on the varsity but saw varsity experience of a sort in practice as members of the "scout" team, which emulated the upcoming opponent.

That year, the Trojans had an all-conference senior wide receiver, Rod Sherman, who went on to play six seasons with five NFL teams.

Obbema was on the scout team, so he had to wear full body protection, which was akin to donning a baseball catcher's protective gear, only with better coverage. The plays run at Obbema and the defense were ones used by Notre Dame, for whom it seems USC always was obsessively preparing.

"As a freshman, I was called out to practice against the varsity, which meant you got the hell beat out of you," he said. "We had a play where Rod Sherman would receive a pass and, as a freshman, I probably couldn't have covered Rod without the protection." But Obbema finally got to Sherman, just as the ball arrived, and tackled him.

"Rod reached down and got me by my face mask and said, 'Nice job, Joey.' Rod Sherman was really an outstanding football player and human being."

That same year, Obbema, playing blocking back in the trademark Trojan I-formation, was part of a super-sized backfield on the freshman team that went 3-0 in games against Stanford, UCLA and Cal when not being pounded by the varsity in practice daily. The other members of the Trobabes backfield included 6-4, 225-pound quarterback Mike Holmgren, who later coached a Super Bowl-winning Green Bay Packers team; 222-pound tailback Fred Khasigian, who became an orthopedic surgeon; and 235-pound fullback Bob Brown, who wound up as an actor known as Reb Brown.

On one other occasion, Goux was cranking out two-handed push-ups, something he did frequently, when McKay sauntered over and dropped down to do 25 one-handed push-ups to intimidate the "intimidator."

One of Obbema's most embarrassing moments as a collegian actually happened in the tie with the Fighting Irish.

"I had a chance to intercept a screen pass in the Notre Dame game, which at the time was tied at 21-21," he said.

The ball was right in Obbema's hands, but he dropped it, when he could have easily walked in to the end zone. A defender grabbed his wrist, pulling the ball out of Obbema's grip.

"I thought that if just would've held on to that ball, we would've beaten Notre Dame. Out of all the football I played, that thing just sticks out in my mind," he sheepishly admitted.

In another game later that same year, he forgot to go on the field for a kickoff, which should have been automatic, being that Obbema was a special teams regular in addition to his defensive-end assignment. But excitement had gotten the better of him after a Trojan touchdown.

"My mom said she had heard it on the radio: 'There's only 10 men on the field, and here comes Obbema; he makes it 11.'"

Obbema termed that tie game as "historic" for an obvious reason.

USC had entered that final regular-season meeting ranked No. 1 nationally and, following the deadlocked result, "that put us No. 2 in the country, and Ohio State No. 1. And that changed the voting of when they could vote for the national championship. Since we were meeting Ohio State and we were No. 2 and they were No. 1, (The

Associated Press) decided to wait and vote on the national championship until after the Rose Bowl game. If we beat Ohio State, we were national champions for the second year in a row," but the Buckeyes preserved their top status by defeating the Trojans in come-from-behind fashion.

"It really was the fair thing to do, and that game was historic for that reason. It was disappointing that we didn't beat them, but they had a very good team, and we had a very good team."

Prior to the fateful 1969 season for Obbema, he was able to enjoy both the on- and off-field humor that is attendant with playing football, especially at the big-school college level and in the pros.

Senior All-America offensive guard Mike Scarpace, for example, unwittingly (or maybe wittingly) provided some of the frivolity. Scarpace was something of an amateur zookeeper, along with some football-playing and non-football-playing fraternity brothers. He kept a pair of *piranhas* – South American man-eating fishes – in his frat-house room; the flesh-eating swimmers were named Abbott and Costello.

One day, Obbema brought a friend to the frat house, and asked Mike where the two fish were. Scarpace replied, "Abbott ate Costello."

Scarpace also was delegated by his fraternity brothers with babysitting an alligator named Flo, which measured almost two feet long.

"We kept it in the boys' shower for a semester. We just named it Flo (or was it Flow?)," he said, not knowing its exact gender. "Then it went under the shower" and someone unknowingly stepped on the reptile, crushing it to death. The fraternity then dressed the dead 'gator in Santa Claus garb, giving it as a Christmas present to a football teammate named Mike Westphal.

Defensive lineman Bill Hayhoe, who was Scarpace's high school and college teammate, is certain from where Scarpace procured the reptile because he had an alligator of his own. "We played at Miami (Fla.) my sophomore year and, at the hotel, in a little gift shop, you could buy these little baby alligators, and they'd send it to you," the 6-foot-8 Hayhoe said. "I had it for a year; I think it got sick" and died. Hayhoe's "pet" was never given a name like Flo/Flow. He was busy falling in love – with a young woman, not the alligator – courting his girlfriend, Debbie, now his wife of 40-plus years.

John G. Smith, one of Obbema's several roommates in the off-campus mock-fraternity house, "Delta Beta," had his own "stewardship" of an alligator when he was growing up in Hollywood, where he attended Hollywood High with such notable classmates as Stefanie Powers, and David and Rick Nelson of *Ozzie and Harriet* fame.

"We kept this baby alligator in the bathtub, and had to take it out any time anyone had to take a bath," Smith said.

Future longtime NFL defensive players Rossovich and Mike Battle were most responsible for providing a lot of the "yuks" around the team. Not coincidentally, both had later roles in Hollywood to different degrees, but before going officially in front of the cameras, they got in their money's worth while still student-athletes, way prior to *Animal House* appearing on movie screens more than a decade later.

"They were the trend-setters," Scarpace said. Their unusual activities included running naked in front of cars long before "streaking" became vogue, eating glass and even jumping off buildings – much to the collective consternation of the Trojan coaching staff. The coaches, you see, could always rely on the pair to perform admirably on the football field; it is just what "Rosso" and Battle did off the field that jangled the coaches' collective nerves.

"They would go to Las Vegas or Palm Springs and stage fights, then take off," said Scarpace, whom Obbema said also was a gifted concert pianist.

Scarpace said his mother was disappointed because he pursued football instead of heading toward the music conservatory. Without bragging, he said self-assuredly he was as good on the piano as Mike Reid, the Penn State All-American and Cincinnati Bengals' talented defensive lineman who gave up football to become a successful full-time singer/songwriter in Nashville. "I originally was a nose guard, but I changed to offense. You can hide your fingers, not like a defensive player," Scarpace said. (Reid, incidentally, followed USC's Ron Yary as Outland Trophy winner as the nation's top interior lineman in 1969, then scored a songwriting Grammy award for Ronnie Milsap's *Stranger in My House* in 1984, followed by a No. 1 country hit with the crossover tune, *Walk on Faith*, in 1990.)

"I've heard him play, and he *really* was good," Trojan center Dick Allmon said regarding Scarpace's inherent ability to finger the ivories.

Allmon lived for some time in one of the rollicking fraternity houses with an often-toxic mixture of athletes and non-athletes. The real *Animal House* was "very tame (compared) to what we did . . . because of the personalities, and it was fairly wild back then," he said.

Strait-laced, self-admitted "square" Steve Grady, the backup to O.J. Simpson, accepted both Rossovich and the smaller, more wiry-muscled Battle as friends, enough so for Rossovich to be a member of Grady's wedding later, saying of him, "he was a good guy."

The 6-foot-5, 250-pound "Rosso," as teammates called him, "drummed his own drums," Grady said. "Battle was a lot like Rossovich, only on a smaller scale," he said of the 6-foot-1, 175-pound defensive back/kick returner. Some of those less charitable toward Battle claimed he merely mimicked Rossovich's original antics.

Both Obbema and John G. Smith recall separate occasions when Rossovich momentarily stopped billiards games by taking one of the balls, lodging it in his mouth, then spitting it out back onto the pool table.

Obbema's son, Matt, was 9 years old when his dad's pal Rossovich wanted to extol the elder Obbema's virtues, so to get Matt's undivided attention, Rosso put him in a friendly headlock until he was finished with his diatribe.

Another time, before Matt met Rossovich for the first time, father and son were watching the movie, *Cloak and Dagger*. Matt, hearing Joe boast about the actor Rossovich on the big screen being a close friend, reckoned that his dad was merely bragging. So he didn't believe the claim until about the time of the headlock when he met Rosso in the flesh.

One Trojan reserve on the '67 team – who asked to remain anonymous – remembers the time when he and Battle, a star starter and prized kick-returner, spent half the night getting drunk in a popular bar just off-campus, and was puzzled at the consequences, which amounted to what the unnamed player felt was a double standard that didn't favor backup performers.

"The next day, Coach McKay called me into his office and warned me that it better not happen again," Battle's previous-night's drinking partner said. "When I asked Battle if McKay had given him a similar warning, he told me nobody had said anything to him. I got the feeling then that they played favorites."

Even without such "crazy men" as Rossovich and Battle, Allmon said that, like most big college football environments, there were enough laughs to go around.

Allmon was a defensive end behind Rossovich in the former's sophomore year before shifting to the other side of the ball. McKay would spend a lot of practice time in a movable tower observing the overall scene. On this particular day, the defensive coaches saw McKay walking down to check the defense. Krueger was the linebackers coach, and he would change to put the second-stringers doing what the first-stringers did. And McKay said to Allmon, referring to him by his last name as was his habit, 'You're so damn dumb, even if there was an earthquake, I'd never play you.'

"Then we beat Clemson in the Coliseum the same day as an earthquake, and I played the whole game," Allmon said.

Also during Allmon's years as a Trojan, he can recall yet another unnamed teammate, this one a defensive lineman who never was inserted into a single game but practiced with the team for five years. In one practice, the unnamed player was doing a drill wrong, and Goux bent down and plunked out a blade of grass. He told him, 'See this blade of grass? It's smarter than you are, and we *knew* you couldn't play at SC.' (Mr. Unnamed) looked up at Goux and said, 'Too bad, I got five years of education out of you.'

Steve Sogge started a number of games at quarterback for the Trojans during his career when the taller Toby Page was injured, and Page in turn spelled him when Sogge was sidelined.

In a home game against Oregon State in the Coliseum in 1968, the year after Page graduated, Sogge was at the controls, guiding the team flawlessly down the field, with star senior tailback Simpson on the shelf with injuries. So, Simpson's super-reliable backup, Grady, was enlisted, down after down, to punch holes in the Beavers' line the same way "Earthquake" Enyart had done to the Trojans the previous year in the thick Corvallis mud.

Sogge called time deep in the visitors' "Red Zone." McKay was furious, slamming his headset and clipboard to the turf hard enough for them to bounce back up into the air slightly. The coach quickly summoned Sogge, demanding to know why he had called time, which stalled the drive temporarily at the Beavers' 5 after a 75-yard march fueled by Grady's rushing.

Being "one of the most intelligent quarterbacks I ever played with," according to Obbema, Sogge patiently listened to his head coach's rant for about 30 seconds, then replied with a grin, "I didn't call timeout; *Grady* called timeout because *he's* tired," Obbema said. It is important to remember that USC entered each game with a game plan centered around Simpson, so, since Grady didn't play as much, as Simpson's backup, he was not necessarily in always as play-ready as the starting tailback.

"Another of McKay's dirty names was horse's ass. He was brutal," said three-year starting guard Steve Lehmer, who knows about this firsthand because he often was referred to as the equine's posterior.

USC had at least four squad members – Lehmer, rover Ty Salness, guard Fred Khasigian and reserve linebacker Bob Jensen -- on the 1967-68 teams who ultimately became doctors or, in one case, a dentist.

The would-be dentist, who not long ago retired from that profession, was Jensen, who obviously was prepared for the future. He was one of the rare football players who wore a protective mouthpiece long before they became a regular safety feature.

At the beginning of the '67 season, Jensen would insert the mouthpiece to protect his teeth. Each time Goux would see the tooth appliance during practice, he would take it away from Jensen and stomp it into the ground. The budding dentist got wise, however, after three or four more times. So when Goux took the next one away, Jensen pulled out another one from under his belt to re-insert in his mouth.

"I guess Coach Goux decided, what the hell, and never bothered him again about it," Obbema said.

Long after their respective college playing careers had ended, Obbema utilized Jensen's professional services at a time of dire dental need. Obbema had lost four front teeth just prior to a scheduled speaking engagement.

"I called Bobby, and asked him if he could replace them," said Obbema, lest he orate in public with his mouth looking like he was a refugee from a

1930s *Grapes of Wrath*-style Dust Bowl camp. "He told me he couldn't do permanent ones but could do temporary ones." Therefore, Obbema was a genuine full-toothed speaker when he appeared in front of the group a few days later.

At times, Obbema still was young enough to be reckless, as his best friend since childhood, Marv "Tink" Hahn, recalls about an incident at the home of Trojan teammate and future NFL and UFL head coach Jim Fassel, who finished his college quarterbacking career at Long Beach State following a brief time at USC.

"Joe and I were at a party at Fassel's parents' house once, and Joe was opening beer bottles with his teeth (before twist-offs); he broke one bottle and didn't know it, so when he went to flick the cap off with his thumb, he split it open to the bone," Hahn said. "He wrapped a towel around it, and he didn't leave the party, although I had a date and had left the party early." Towels must have been in long supply in that household because Fassel's dad was equipment manager at Anaheim High, and his uncle, Chick Flynn, had the same job at Anaheim's archrival, Western, Hahn's old school.

Regarding the bottle-cap incident, "I vaguely remember that," said Fassel, who coached the Las Vegas Locomotive to the first two championships of the fledgling United Football League in 2009 and 2010, beating the Florida Tuskers in each case. The UFL teams had an abbreviated 2011 season, with Las Vegas losing the championship game to the Virginia Destroyers, before the league folded.

Fassel also was head coach when the New York Giants won the NFC East divisional championship in 2000 and was named NFL Coach of the Year in 1997. Since he was coaching the Giants when the Twin Towers were attacked by Islamic terrorists, Fassel initiated The Jim Fassel Foundation to help families of 9/11 victims who have incurred unexpected expenses.

"Joe was always a personality guy, a guy's guy, the life of the party," Fassel said, adding that Obbema perpetually has possessed an inherent loyalty. "You always knew, could tell, that he'd have your back."

Fassel, one of a number of former NFL head coaches and assistant coaches who have called Obbema a good friend, firmly believes that Obbema had "the ability, toughness and attitude" to have had a successful pro football career, had he not been seriously injured in his senior year as a Trojan.

A USC assistant coach who came to Troy after Obbema stopped playing was Wayne Fontes, who later went on to become the most successful head coach in Detroit Lions' history, during the Barry Sanders era.

It wasn't long after Fontes's arrival at University Park, however, that he and Obbema took a quick shine to each other.

"Joe's one of the great guys – highly thought of by the coaching staff," Fontes said. "Joe was a legend at SC; the stories about him ..." from his playing days, when he always helped coaches recruit high school seniors with his tough-guy/soft-heart mixture of charm, and for years thereafter as an unofficial Trojan "ambassador."

"The way people (perceive of) him . . . Mister SC. . . . He would do anything in the Trojan Family," Fontes said. "He was a *real* person; no bull shit; if you needed something, talk to Joe."

He and other coaches would sit around for hours and listen to Obbema's stories, said Fontes, now retired and living in Tarpon Springs, Fla., a small community settled originally by Greek fishermen near Tampa. "We've all spread to different parts of the country, and have managed to keep in touch over the years," he said.

It was Wayne Fontes who introduced Obbema to colorful former Chicago Bears' head man Abe Gibron. Gibron had been the Bears' coach when running back Brian Piccolo died of cancer, as well documented in the book and 1971 television movie, *Brian's Song*, in which the well-fed coach portrayed himself.

"We hit it off real well" from the outset, Obbema said. "Abe used to come in to Julie's Restaurant (just off-campus) for SC games."

Julie's, named after founder/proprietor Julie Kohl, who died at age 98 in 2002, according to her obituary in the *Los Angeles Times*, was actually two places just off-campus: Julie's Restaurant at 37th and Flower streets, and Julie's Trojan Barrel just down the block at 37th and Figueroa. While both, which closed within two years of each other in 1997 and 1999, according to a 1999 *Trojan Chronicle* account, were obvious Trojan hangouts, they also attracted numerous non-USC *glitterati* from nearby Hollywood.

John Mitchell, longtime defensive line coach and assistant head coach for the Pittsburgh Steelers, had been recruited by USC out of Eastern Arizona (Junior) College four decades ago. So in the "bum's rush" of recruitment – which always included "Ambassador" Obbema, it seems – he visited Julie's, before he eventually transferred from the Arizona school to Alabama to play for the late Paul "Bear" Bryant's Crimson Tide in Mitchell's native state. By doing so, Mitchell, an African-American, broke the color line at 'Bama and wound up eventually being inducted into the Alabama Hall of Fame.

"Julie's was the best place in Southern California because you'd have no idea about who you'd run across," said Mitchell, 62, who has been a National Football League assistant coach for three decades, the last 19 years with the Steelers, earning two Super Bowl rings, the most recent in 2009.

One would bet that, when the Tide rolled into the L.A. Coliseum to play USC the year after Mitchell signed on with Bryant, he surely must have talked the coaching legend into letting him eat at Julie's or the Trojan Barrel.

Mitchell said of Obbema, "Joe's the type of guy who, if he's your friend, he's your friend through thick and thin, unless you don't know him, (then) he can rub you the wrong way" – which aptly describes Joe Obbema's soft-hard character mix.

No doubt that Obbema ever rubbed the late Abe Gibron the wrong way, and it was at Julie's, of course, where that friendship more or less germinated.

The portly Gibron was a noted lover of food, as attested to by a former Tampa Bay Buccaneer rookie quoted in a 1977 *Sports Illustrated* story. Charley Hannah, Mitchell's fellow former Tide player, said after dining with Gibron, who was a Tampa Bay assistant coach, "He was eating things we wouldn't even go swimming with in Alabama." In short, Abe Gibron was a *gourmand* – and a grateful one, at that – as evidenced by what occurred not long after the initial meeting with Obbema at Julie's.

(It should be mentioned that Bob Obradovich and family, who bought the original Julie's from Kohl in her later years while Kohl kept the Trojan Barrel, thought so much of Obbema, and vice-versa, that one of the Special Event menu items was re-named the "Joe Obbema Teriyaki Chicken Char-Broiled Boneless Breast" [with rice and a veggie side], priced at $9.95. Obbema was worried that Trojan and Steeler receiving great Lynn Swann might have been "pissed off" since the chicken entrée originally bore Swann's name. The

Obradoviches, whose oldest son, Jim, played tight end for nine seasons in the NFL after a USC apprenticeship, also had food items named after Nick Pappas ["Mr. Trojan"], Jon Arnett, Craig Fertig and walk-on footballer Seamus Callanan [one of 24 part-time bartenders at Julie's, most of whom were of-age Trojan football players]. Other items were named for present or former USC athletes, most notably John Wayne, who had starred in football as a Trojan many years previously under his given name of Marion "Duke" Morrison. Coincidentally, Wayne played at the university behind the future *Wagon Train* wagon master and classic character actor, Ward Bond, who in turn introduced the young Morrison/Wayne to the Hollywood crowd.)

"I told him about PJ Macaluso, who owned a restaurant and Advantage Sports, a travel agency that Abe wanted to use for travel," Obbema said of Gibron. So Obbema and Macaluso, who also was a world-class chef, treated Gibron to dinner at the upscale Italian *ristorante* Manhattan of La Jolla inside that posh suburb's snazzy Empress Hotel near San Diego. Macaluso, a New York transplant, was co-owner and executive chef of Manhattan of La Jolla.

"Abe probably never paid for a meal in his life, but the meal was so good that he came back with three friends and paid for it himself." (As testament to Obbema's ongoing incredible networking ability, *he* had originally met Macaluso through the Los Angeles Rams' Hall of Fame "Fearsome Foursome" member David "Deacon" Jones – probably at Julie's; Jones died in late spring 2013 at age 74.)

Jim Obradovich said that, before Gibron died of a stroke in 1997, he was a scout for the Seattle Seahawks and, every time he was in Los Angeles, he would drop by Julie's for memories and meals.

Matt Obbema said that in his pre-teen years, when he walked into Julie's with his father, he felt like he had entered a taping for the old television situation comedy, *Cheers*, because, he said, "everybody would know (Joe's name)."

In Kohl's newspaper obituary, the importance of Julie's was underscored: *"McKay always held court at Booth No. 1, where he plotted plays and gabbed with his coaching staff and any reporter who pulled up a chair. When McKay left to coach the NFL's Tampa Bay Buccaneers, Kohl had his booth dismantled and shipped to Tampa Bay, where it was installed in his new restaurant hangout."*

"I spent many a good time in that booth with John McKay," radio sportscaster Tom Kelly fondly remembers. Kelly's association with the Trojans goes back to 1961, the year after McKay was hired as head coach.

That new culinary haunt in Tampa, according to Wayne Fontes, was Malio's, which was a longtime landmark on busy Dale Mabry Highway for years until it closed in 2005. Owner Malio Iavarone and his son, Derek, then opened Malio's Prime Steakhouse in 2007 on the ground floor of a tall bank building in downtown Tampa, directly across the Hillsborough River from the historic, Victorian- and Moorish-flavored University of Tampa, and not far from the Bucs' Raymond James Stadium. Fontes said the old Malio's "was like Julie's; the same type." Jim Obradovich, who played on the same squad as Charley Hannah, said that Bucs' players were not allowed to patronize Malio's because alcoholic beverages were sold there.

One has to surmise that, since Abe Gibron coached under McKay with the Buccaneers after his Chicago tenure, he doubtless spent many munching moments in Malio's Booth No. 1, transplanted from Julie's. Yet the big question, if you believe Hannah, is: Did old Abe eat from the menu or otherwise?

The original Malio's also played an eventual role in another episode involving ex-Trojans.

Obbema was joined on a business trip to the Tampa Bay area by ex-assistant coach Craig Fertig so that they could visit with their former head coach, McKay, already retired from coaching but still living in that area after being the Buccaneers' inaugural field general.

"Coach said he would have his wife, Corky, pick us up at the airport. Craig had arranged for us to stay at the Airport Sheraton," Obbema said. When the two picked up their bags and were waiting outside for Corky McKay, up drove John McKay instead, prompting a pair of nearby local businessmen to comment to Obbema and Fertig, "You guys really have a high-priced driver."

McKay informed them to hurry up because of an impending tee time, which he didn't want to miss. In his haste to get to the golf course on time, the witty retired coach broke several traffic laws, then told his former Trojan buddies that he would return later to pick them up for dinner at Malio's. After McKay left, Fertig and Obbema attempted to check in but were informed that their hotel was actually attached to the airport, to which they would have to go back.

"I never let Fertig make arrangements again," Obbema vowed.

When McKay returned to pick up the pair, they were escorted at Malio's into a very private room that was one of only three special niches set aside by Malio Iavarone, a gregarious, gray-haired second-generation Italian-American Tampa native who had grown up in the same neighborhood as colorful baseball manager Lou Piniella. One room was earmarked for then-San Francisco 49ers' owner Eddie DeBartolo, a second for the late New York Yankees' owner George Steinbrenner, a longtime Tampa resident, and the other for McKay, including the booth Julie Kohl had shipped to Tampa for her favorite head coach. (Iavarone re-installed the same booth in his new steakhouse in 2007 and used it as a prototype for other booths at the latter location. Following the Yankees' 2009 World Series victory, good-pal Steinbrenner rewarded Iavarone with a giant Series ring that the restaurateur proudly wears on his left ring finger.)

While McKay and Obbema – who coincidentally shared July 5 as a birthdate – were enjoying dinner and drinks with Fertig, two Buccaneer boosters stopped by and, although McKay no longer was coaching at Tampa Bay, said they wanted to merely say hi. That prompted McKay to tap into Obbema's inherent story-telling ability and have his loquacious ex-player relate an anecdote about the 1967 championship team.

Understand that a major part of that tale-telling talent was using his hands, which led to the drinks being knocked from the waitress's grip by Obbema's gesticulation into his old coach's lap.

"For a moment, I thought I was 19 years old again, and thought I was going to have to run laps or something," Obbema said. As the waitress was cleaning up the mess after Obbema's apology and McKay telling him in turn not to worry, the ex-coach lit up one of his trademark cigars and, turning to Fertig, said, "You know, Craig, that's the first time one of my players ever cold-cocked me," causing everyone to share a laugh.

There's an old saying in the NFL: "Telephone, telegraph, tell a coach" – meaning that if you tell a good story to one coach, before long everyone will have heard it.

That was the case the next day following the drink-spillage incident when Obbema called old friend Fontes to relate to him what had happened. Soon afterward – about 48 hours later – Obbema and Fertig were on a three-hour layover at the Atlanta airport, where they were in a bar watching the murder trial of former teammate O.J. Simpson on TV.

"Craig said, 'You won't believe who is walking this way,' and in comes Coach Mike Holmgren," another of Obbema's USC ex-teammates. Holmgren told Obbema he wanted to give him a high-five and, when Obbema inquired as to why, the then-Green Bay Packers' head coach said, for cold-cocking McKay. It had taken only 48 hours for another "tell-a" story to get legs.

While Obbema said it is always great to see former fellow squad members in person after many years, he had a special affection for Holmgren, whom he regards as "one of the greatest coaches and motivators in history." The two, of course, were backfield mates on USC's 1966 freshman squad.

(Incidentally, speaking of Atlanta's Hartsfield-Jackson airport, which is the world's busiest, in the latest rankings, residents from all over the Southeast will tell you without hesitation, "When you die, whether you go to Heaven or Hell, you still have to make a connection through Hartsfield.")

Ninety-seven-year-old Nick Pappas's pedigree as Mr. Trojan goes way back to his playing days in the 1930s before he went on to become an assistant football coach and associate athletic director. Pappas was as much a regular as McKay or anyone else at Julie's, so he had certain special privileges.

"I would be there with four or five guys, and she'd charge the other guys, but wouldn't charge me," said Pappas, who surmises that the already good USC football program had the most-positive turning point in its storied history when McKay was hired as head coach in 1960. In 16 seasons, before departing for Tampa Bay, he proceeded to lead the Trojans to four national championships and nine conference titles.

As many hours as campus denizens spent at Julie's and the Trojan Barrel – which were numerous -- there were other ways to procure meals in those days for USC athletes, non-athletes, undergraduates, graduate students and assorted hangers-on alike.

"We also hung around at the 901 Club, especially Thursday night, because they had a burger special," said John G. Smith, a California native who earned a Ph.D. in Physical Education at USC after already having gotten his Master's at the University of Illinois. (Smith today runs a fitness and wellness center at Long Beach City College, hopefully schooling his charges on better nutritional habits than he and his sidekicks practiced in the boys-will-be-boys atmosphere of the '60s.)

The other places where they ate included the 32nd Street Market, Maury's and a joint where they would order "garbage" burritos with no beans. "Those were our diet," said Smith, who was a fellow bouncer with Obbema as well as one of 10 roommates in the mock-frat house. There also was a pick-up bar, Rosie's, with the same owner as a similar establishment called Mom's that served students across town at archrival UCLA in Westwood. "Rosie's was about one-tenth the size of Mom's, almost a mockery of Mom's at UCLA," Smith said.

The fake-frat boys also would gamble to determine who would do sandwich runs. Additionally, when the fellows were not inclined to "order out," there was a rather handy way to eat in by earning a meal at Delta Beta, which incidentally was "Greek" shorthand for "Dead Beat." "We had a rule if you couldn't find a dish to use, you had to do the dishes" from a pile of dirty dinnerware that had stacked up around the kitchen, Smith said. But there still was even more from a so-called culinary standpoint.

Two resident dogs -- a black Labrador named Odin and a shepherd mix named Tonya – shared the DB house. "We put up a plank and punched a hole in the wall to give the dogs access to the house." Smith said.

Once, a sorority had saved scraps for the dogs' dinner – in a big bag. Inside, there were untouched steaks, prime rib and pieces that were not just your normal throwaways, so the DB boys cooked the "scraps" and ate them themselves.

Then there was the day Odin went missing for a few hours, but his dog tags must have saved him.

"We went out front and started yelling, 'Odin, Odin.' Some baseball players were coming back to the Row from practice, and heard us. They said a dog named Odin had been shagging balls at practice," Smith said of the mock-frat house that sat on Fraternity Row closer to campus than the legitimately registered Greek residences.

The DB boys had a fairly easy way to pay their monthly rent during Obbema's senior year – the period when he resided there. He had spent a year each respectively as a sophomore and junior, first in an on-campus dormitory with a non-athlete roommate, then in an off-campus house with other non-sports living partners.

"Every Friday we'd have a kegger party" at Delta Beta. "We'd charge a couple of bucks a head, and we made our rent that way," Obbema said. For a semester before he moved in to the Delta Beta house primarily with John Loomis and John G. Smith, Obbema roomed with teammate Bill Brucker, who had been played with fellow Trojans Scarpace and Hayhoe at Birmingham High in Van Nuys.

"Bill was one of those players who, like Ron Yary had said, never got the chance to suit up but was always there for practices," Obbema said. Brucker became a police officer and eventually a detective in the seaside city of Santa Monica.

The life trajectory of one of the players for the 1967-68 Trojans, the late defensive line reserve Doug Mooers, is illustrative – at least in his widow Barbara's mind. Mooers practiced and suited up all season in '67 after transferring from Air Force but was forbidden by NCAA transfer rules from being allowed to play in games. He did, however, play in every game in 1968.

"Since I own a company that sells equipment to waste-water treatment plants, my wife likes to tell people my career path was the Rose Bowl to the Super Bowl to the Toilet Bowl," said Mooers before passing away in 2011. He also played three years of pro football in Dallas, New Orleans and St. Louis before settling eventually in the Milwaukee, Wis., suburbs.

Unfortunately for Joe Obbema, events occurring around him turned less funny for a while, beginning at the end of the 1968 campaign.

After two seasons lettering as a sophomore and junior, he played part of the 1969 opener at Nebraska but sat out the rest of his senior year due to injuries initially incurred in practice as his junior season closed out, yet the problems were aggravated in the Cornhusker game, which USC won. That victory was *Pyrrhic* for Obbema, though, because the injury occurred on a play on which he was charged with a personal foul.

"I got a piling-on penalty, and the coaches were really upset with me," he said. ". . . I hurt my right shoulder and it put me out for the rest of the season, but I got to suit up in the ('70) Rose Bowl game due to Coach McKay's kindness.

"Nebraska, to us, was not the powerhouse that Coach McKay knew they were," Obbema said. So McKay took his team back there a day early, just to prove a point. "Nebraska's stadium is kind of like Ohio State's: kind of a horseshoe type of thing. So we were walking the field Friday afternoon, and he said, 'I want to show you how serious people feel about football back here,' and he took us over to where the parking lot was."

An estimated 40,000 people had already gathered in the parking lot – on Friday afternoon for a Saturday game! – for what would amount to overnight "tailgating."

As impressive as it was, that gathering, of course, was nothing compared to the 76,000-plus that would pack Memorial Stadium the following day, making the arena the third-largest city in the state for one day – smaller than only Omaha and Lincoln.

A similar fate beset Obbema's classmate and fellow Orange Countian, Lehmer, who became another "Broken Trojan" during the 1969 season. Injuries forced his playing time to be greatly reduced after the Notre Dame game, the fifth of the season and a 14-14 road tie following four consecutive wins to open the season.

USC finished 10-0-1 and capped the season with the '70 Rose Bowl win over Michigan to rate No. 5 in the final national rankings behind Texas, Penn State, Arkansas and Ohio State.

"I had a great first two years, then broke my ankle/tore ligaments the day before the start of Rose Bowl practice for Ohio State 1969," Lehmer said. "They had me all shot up anyway . . . with Xylocaine and painkillers. I had a decent game despite the loss."

Lehmer was strongly urged to have surgery and redshirt the next year, but turned down surgery – "foolishly, and a mistake," he said – and did not want to redshirt. He could never again perform certain maneuvers due to the unstable ankle, and had an unsatisfactory senior year. He even lost his starting-guard position after the Notre Dame game that year, and was not drafted by the NFL.

"It was devastating to me and hard to deal with, but resulted in my pursuit of medicine thereafter. One good thing, though, was that I *was* drafted by the Army, and failed the Army physical because of my crippled ankle, thus staying out of Vietnam, where I probably would have been killed, knowing me," Lehmer said. "I eventually had the ankle surgery 26 years later, after getting tired of it rolling out of joint and throwing me to the ground, and it has been fine ever since."

Like Obbema, Lehmer had the possibility of playing pro football dangled in front of him.

"I always wanted to be a doctor, and was thinking about whether I could do it . . . then I wasn't drafted (by the NFL)," Lehmer said. "I tried out with the (Oakland) Raiders. I saw Gene Upshaw at a workout, and he was two steps ahead of everybody else – big, fast and quick, just like (USC teammate and future Hall of Famer Ron) Yary." Upshaw, who also was elected to the Pro Football Hall of Fame, distinguished himself later in the challenging role as the respected long-standing executive director of the NFL Players Association before his death in 2008.

Lehmer laughs now reflectively as he ponders how that experience hastened his actual fate. He said it really made him want to go into the medical profession. But Lehmer's similarly interesting life story could be an entirely separate book by itself someday, it seems. After all, he spent an estimated additional 18 years of post-graduate education en route to his career as a physician and surgeon.

As for Obbema, one of his coaches his senior year at Mater Dei High School was Notre Dame alumnus Jim Martin, a linebacker/place-kicker with the Detroit Lions who had set an NFL record with a 53-yard field goal. Martin helped arrange a free-agent tryout for him with the Lions, but it never materialized, mostly for physical reasons related to the lingering serious shoulder injury that had initially been incurred in practice at the end of Obbema's junior year. Doctors reasoned that his shoulder could not weather the constant pounding anymore.

"When you're 21, you think it's gonna go on forever. You think you're gonna play until you're 60," Obbema said. Then you discover reality, couched by the pure physical inability to accomplish what used to be routine – and you proceed on an entirely different life's path.

Obbema then shifted mental gears to face the rest of *his* life without playing his beloved game, yet the constants remained: The big guy with the gruff exterior continued to use his huge heart to help the downtrodden and those generally less fortunate – in varied ways and despite his own personal tragedies.

Chuck Dekeado, who was a longtime unofficial advisor to John McKay, believes Obbema was one of several Trojans whose fondness for the "training table" (code for the abundant food choices available in dormitories and those other off-campus places where perpetually hungry football players congregated) slowed them down. He concedes, for example, that Obbema went from 225 pounds to 245 at USC, mainly due to the culinary cornucopia.

"Back then, it was before there were fitness and training coordinators," Dekeado said, so players didn't pay as close attention as today to diets and nutrition – to wit: Such "delicacies" as the aforementioned garbage burrito.

Regardless of what may have slowed him down – figuratively or literally – anyone who *really* knows Joe Obbema is convinced that, had he not been sidelined by injuries, he possessed the talent and desire to have eventually enjoyed a fruitful career in pro football (probably as a linebacker), just as good friend and master talent-evaluator Jim Fassel had mentioned.

5

THE USC 'WILD BUNCH' MEETS

THE *REAL* WILD BUNCH

Made us nobly wild, not mad.

-- Hesperides, Ode for Ben Jonson, Robert Herrick
(1591-1674)

The USC Trojan football players, especially the defensive linemen, had a penchant for watching movies – either films of their past games, sneak-peeks at upcoming opponents or simply enjoying full-length Hollywood offerings. After all, most of the Tinseltown flicks were made largely just a few miles from campus, and quite likely were produced by fellow University of Southern California graduates.

During one of those various film sessions, someone at some point (no one knows exactly when and who) agreed while watching director Sam Peckinpah's entertaining, violent Western, *The Wild Bunch*, that this particular piece of cinematic entertainment was applicable to the big defenders.

Probably the most likely candidate for "marrying" the movie cowboys with the Trojan heroes was the late assistant football coach, Marv Goux, widely renowned as "Mr. Spirit" for inspirational speeches to the team. Goux (pronounced GOO), who died in 2002, one day watched *The Wild Bunch* with his players, then got up and proclaimed afterward, "The objective of defense is to seek out the ball-carrier and separate him from the ball. Warner Brothers should consider our group for its next Western," according to USC's official athletic website.

Therefore, from then on, a half-dozen or so USC defensive line stalwarts somehow came to be known as The Wild Bunch. The primary players were Al Cowlings, the late Willard "Bubba" Scott, Tody Smith, Charley Weaver and Jimmy Gunn. Those were the five Trojans, all African-American "cowboys," decked out in Western duds, in the famous picture donated by Goux's widow, Patricia, that still hangs in the USC athletic archives. Sometimes-Bunchers included Gary McArthur, Tony Terry and a guy named Joe Obbema.

"Because I got hurt, I wasn't a part of that," Obbema said of the core group of the Wild Bunch. "That really bothered me" since he was so close personally to the Bunch's members, with whom he practiced daily.

A life-size, bronze sculpture of the five main Wild Bunchers, provided to USC by an anonymous donor, was placed outside the on-campus Heritage Hall in 2002. All five earned some form of All-Conference or All-America status during their Trojan playing careers.)

Although Obbema was not a regular on the USC crew – especially after injuries prevented him from playing most of his senior year in 1969, in the many years after graduation and earning his teaching certificate -- he constantly faced off against those who could be easily regarded as the *real, live* Wild Bunch. Those other rowdies were a long way from the campus and potentially much more lethal in a truly lawless sense.

Even before he took on extra jobs for nearly three years as a bouncer near Hollywood and at different locations in what Southern Californians know as the Beach Cities (especially Manhattan Beach and Torrance), Joe Obbema still found himself in characteristic fashion – mostly protecting the more-vulnerable from bullying types but also occasionally winding up in, well, interesting, unusual, and even embarrassing situations.

"For the whole time, he was the toughest guy," roommate and bouncing colleague John G. Smith said of Obbema. "The thing about him as a friend, if you messed with one of us, you messed with all of us. There was nothing he wouldn't do for you as a friend." Smith termed the relationship as the strongest form of bonding that was possible.

Some of the members of Delta Beta, the mock-fraternity that the 10 residents of their shared house had created, "were the toughest guys at SC, so nobody would complain about it," Smith said. About one weekend a month, they would rent out the house for a sorority's T-G-I-F, and there were many parties, including something called skip-go-naked. The girls would provide the pizza and kegs, the latter which became makeshift furniture for the abode.

Among assorted other hi-jinks were head-butting contests in front of the house; a pipe-throwing competition, tossing a 20-pound "spear" into the walls; and hosting players from Trojan opponents who would get drunk and admit, after a few beers, that they marveled as to how the big USC linemen were faster than their own running backs and receivers.

"One night, we pulled out all the bushes" (literally the plants growing outside, *not* the figurative usage for a specific female body part) at a neighboring sorority house during some sorority sisters' initiation, Smith said.

Activities, however, were not limited to the Delta Beta house, where Obbema resided his senior year. Other than some occasional off-campus locales closer to his boyhood Orange County home, Obbema lived mostly from freshmen through junior years in varied apartments or dormitories, largely with non-athlete roommates.

A sorority sister for whom Obbema had a particular fondness was his girlfriend for awhile his senior year, "Teddy" Kendall.

"On Valentine's Day, they put up a sign that said 'Obbema Valentine.' That was really fun," he said.

Meanwhile, because he could no longer play college football, Obbema also focused on his studies en route to earning a Bachelor of Science degree in Marketing. Yet the coaches also utilized his outgoing personality to help charm high school seniors into believing that USC was the best place to continue their football pursuits.

Serving as an ambassador-of-Troy, Obbema reached out to help recruit potential future stars, including the bevy of talented football players who had followed him at Mater Dei.

Obbema boasts a laudable track record in that regard, claiming initially that his alma mater's High School All-America defensive lineman, Eric Patton, "was the only recruit I lost," then quickly correcting himself: "Two other guys I lost became very famous baseball players," to which Obbema would further allude later. Much to the "ambassador's" dismay, and despite his best efforts, Patton defected to the intersectional enemy, Notre Dame, where he had a storied gridiron career.

It wasn't Joe Obbema's fault, however, according to Patton; it was simply acceding to the wishes of Patton's very Catholic mother, who couldn't envision her 6-foot-2, 200-pound-plus linebacker-son anyplace but Notre Dame.

"My dad was very much in favor of me playing at Stanford. Coach John Ralston had a great staff with (Jim) Mora (the elder) and (Dick) Vermeil (both future NFL head coaches)," said Patton, now 63 and a longtime head football coach in his native

Orange County. "Plus, my dentist was from Stanford. I had a devout Catholic mom and had gone to St. Anne's school and Mater Dei. She was very quiet and reserved," but her wishes spoke for themselves by loudly and unreservedly prevailing, Patton added.

The mustachioed Patton, who has been head football coach at San Clemente High School the past decade-plus, also guided nearby Capistrano Valley to the California Interscholastic Southern Section title in1990. He recalls with gusto Obbema's efforts but admits his heart always was set on being a member of the Fighting Irish, even though it also placated Patton's mother.

"I was very much taken by Joe, but it wasn't just Joe . . . but Coach Dick Coury was also at USC," Patton said. Coury had developed an unintended, almost saint-like status among the players he had coached at Mater Dei because he enjoyed a special knack for treating them like human beings and regular people rather than mere football machines.

With that approach, Coury basked in continual success in drawing out the best from already talented performers, regardless of position.

(There is a tale told by more than one former player of the United States Football League's New Orleans Breakers that, on several occasions, Head Coach Coury would have a players-only, ice-cold beer keg placed conveniently in one end zone after a hard practice. Coury himself, though, never has been a big drinker.)

Despite his desire to suit up as a member of the Fighting Irish, Patton nonetheless realized the value he was forfeiting by forsaking USC.

"It was a real natural fit, and I always looked up to Joe," he said. "He was two years my senior and (on) the CIF championship team (Mater Dei won the Southern Section title in 1965), and he was a real leader, and I wanted to play with him at USC."

Back then, before the National Collegiate Athletic Association, college football's governing body, began cracking down on the number of personal visits a recruit was allowed, Patton enjoyed the competition for his services.

"That was back in the day . . . you could go out and be wined and dined" with no limitations on personal visits, he said. (The latter-day spin on recruiting is underscored in Michael Lewis's book, *The Blind Side*, and its award-winning film adaptation, where a typically pushy NCAA enforcement official comes across none-too-well.)

Patton eventually graduated from Notre Dame – coincidentally, Coury's alma mater – with a degree in English (which he teaches today in addition to coaching), then went on to play with the old World Football League's Southern California Sun after having been drafted by the NFL's Green Bay Packers. He last saw Obbema in the fall of 2009 at an 80th birthday party for Coury organized by the Mater Dei Lettermen's Club and spearheaded by ex-Monarch John Heffernan.

"There were 40 guys at Coach Coury's 80th birthday party. It was down at the San Clemente Pier, the restaurant there. It was quite a testament to the kind of guy and coach he was," Obbema said.

As with nearly everyone else associated over the years with Obbema, Patton said of his Monarch predecessor, whom he backed up on defense when Patton was a sophomore and Obbema a senior, "He's definitely a tough guy . . . and a guy you don't mess around with . . . (but) he has a big heart," accurately assessing both sides of Obbema's complex personality.

Well before the national championship season, Obbema already was assisting John McKay and the other coaches in coaxing recruits into wearing the Cardinal-and-Gold.

The timing, however, was not always advantageous. A prime example was when Obbema innocently escorted a trio of prospects to what turned out to be a 51-0 loss to Notre Dame at the Coliseum in 1966.

"Coach McKay had stressed the importance of beating Notre Dame . . . and I was trying to help recruit three Fullerton Junior College players," Obbema said. He brought the Fullerton trio to the unfortunate debacle against the Irish and it was probably the score, not the company, which spooked them away. The three, running back Clem Crum from Fullerton High, tight end Dennis Dixon from Orange High and defensive back Bob Abbott from Anaheim High, were teammates of Obbema's best friend, tackle Marv "Tink" Hahn, on a Fullerton Hornets squad that had beaten Henderson, Texas, in the Junior Rose Bowl the previous year. None of the threesome, however, opted for USC.

"Dixon went to Alabama as a tight end and captain, Abbott went to Miami as a safety, and Crum went into the Army as a private," Hahn said. Crum was so fast on that Junior Rose Bowl team,

Hornet fans often would chant, "Give it to Crum and let him run."

Tink Hahn also recalls another isolated incident that occurred while his best buddy was leaving a restaurant in Buena Park, close to where Obbema grew up and, as an adult, later lived in a different house from that owned by his parents. Hahn got a phone call one night about his best friend. Two ruffians had jumped Obbema coming out of Denny's restaurant near famous theme park Knott's Berry Farm, and he broke one guy's jaw and the other guy's leg in retaliation. "I later asked Joe how he knew he broke the guy's jaw," Hahn said. "He said, matter-of-factly, 'I felt it break when I hit him'." And what about the other attacker's leg? Hahn said that Obbema replied, again without a blink, 'I curb-stomped his femur.'

"It's true," Obbema confirmed. "They jumped me because I told them to stop giving the (5-foot-2) waitress a hard time." Obbema did not realize it at the time, but the incident proved a precursor to a future avocation which required use of his fists.

While Obbema, still a teen-ager himself, was courting Patton, the three Hornets and so many others, he wound up experiencing what he regarded as his greatest highlight as a young athlete and fan, and, remarkably, it did not happen on the football field. But it did involve the two "very famous baseball players" to whom he had referred when discussing his pursuit of Patton.

"When I look back, I think about what John Hall, a sports columnist for the *L.A. Times*, asked me right after we beat UCLA, 21-20," Obbema said. Hall was interviewing O.J. Simpson, in the next dressing stall, and he turned to Obbema and said, 'This must be the greatest moment of your life' – which it *was* for a game, but the greatest moment overall for Obbema, he told Hall, was meeting baseball managing and coaching greats Casey Stengel and Rod Dedeaux, a tidbit that Hall included in his column.

". . . I was trying to help recruit Bill Buckner and Bobby Valentine, who wanted to play both baseball and football at SC. They were both great football players and baseball players. While we were watching the SC-Stanford baseball game, Tommy Lasorda and Al Campanis walked up," Obbema said. Lasorda, who still was managing Triple-A Albuquerque at the time, was later to craft a Hall of Fame managing career with the Los Angeles Dodgers, and the late Campanis, who died in 1998, was a high-ranking executive with the parent ballclub. "We were watching the game, and Bobby was admiring the radio Tommy Lasorda had brought with him. So Lasorda gave it to him. *We* couldn't do things like that because NCAA rules prohibited it." However, someone like Lasorda was able to offer such a gift because he was not officially affiliated with any college program.

About three weeks later, Valentine, Boston Red Sox manager in 2012, and Buckner were 1-2 in the Major League Baseball draft. Obbema, only 19 at the time, and a youthful contingent of Trojans went up to the suburban Glendale house of Dedeaux, the late, iconic Trojan baseball coach, for brunch.

"We look over, and (longtime New York Yankees' manager and Dedeaux'sfellow Glendale resident) Stengel was there, and he was just staring, talking about the 1927 Yankees – you know, Lou Gehrig, Babe Ruth. Coach Dedeaux never called anyone by their first name; he called everyone Tiger. He came over to me and said, 'Tiger, take the boys to go get something to eat, and then you can come back over to get a lesson from Casey.'"

On reflection, Obbema said, *that* very brief encounter with the "Ol' Perfesser," as Stengel was called, was, as he had related to John Hall, the greatest moment of his life up to that point, along with breaking bread with a coaching great like Dedeaux; the UCLA win was his greatest moment in a *game* situation.

"When you meet a guy like Casey Stengel, you're immediately impressed by that, a person of such magnitude. At 19," he said, with awe still in his voice more than four decades later, "you don't really realize how many great people you're around . . . and how many people I was lucky enough to meet. You don't realize what a great coach Coach McKay was, or how great Coach Coury was."

Simply having been a Trojan football letterman had its perks, and drawbacks – in and around Los Angeles, it seems. That and the repeated bittersweet aspects of Joe Obbema's life were further illustrated in events that soon followed.

Obbema had bought a '65 Mustang that was very popular model at that time. He was driving the car back from his parents' house before two-a-day practices started. It was raining, and he became involved in a 56-car pileup on the Santa Ana (I-5)

Freeway near the Atlantic exit southeast of downtown Los Angeles. His car was about eighth or ninth in the chain-reaction accident.

Obbema tried to slow down but his car slid sideways, plus those were pre-safety belt days. The main portion of the mishap was across the median on the other side of the freeway. He dove and collided with the windshield, cursing under his breath, "Dammit, I broke the windshield," realizing later that the car was totaled anyway.

Then he carefully exited the Mustang, noticing another male driver, whose Jeep had hit a truck so hard that the impact knocked the man's engine into the passenger compartment with the driver bleeding profusely.

Obbema ran over, and tried to open the Jeep's door, and when he pulled on the door handle, he tore it off. "So I reached and grabbed the little window and pulled the guy out," he said. With the rescued man still in his grasp, Obbema saw a truck careening toward them, so he took the man he had rescued and dove behind the exit sign to avoid further injury. The truck landed flat on top of the man's Jeep, and Obbema and the Jeep driver were transported to the hospital, Obbema sustaining a cut on his head and other minor injuries.

"Coach McKay saw the whole thing on the TV news" and Obbema said the head man almost went into an apoplectic fit.

By the time Obbema returned to the mock-fraternity house where he lived near campus in the middle of the night, one of his roommates, a prankster, happened to answer the phone when a reporter called.

"The reporter asked if I was OK, and my friend, said, 'Don't you know? He'll never play again.' And he puts on this guy again for about 10 minutes, telling him how screwed up I am, and he can hear a typewriter in the background. Then when the reporter asked if there was anything else, my friend laughed and told him, 'What I just told you was bull shit. Don't ever call here at 2:30 in the morning again.'"

Obbema actually recovered without any interruption in playing time.

Jon Loomis said that, when he, Obbema and John G. Smith resided together as primary roommates with seven other fellow male roomies in the rented Delta Beta house just off Frat Row, "we formed our own 'fraternity' house. We painted Delta and Beta symbols on the side of the house," he said. "The Deltas and Betas were on campus, so we 'joined' both," said Loomis, a former USC defensive lineman who for a year had attended Dartmouth College, an Ivy League school in western New Hampshire from which his father had graduated.

While he shared living space with Obbema and Smith and the others, Loomis worked as a bouncer off Wilshire Boulevard's storied Miracle Mile, just due south of Hollywood and several miles west of downtown Los Angeles, at an interesting place known as The Garage. As would be the case later at Cisco's in Manhattan Beach's popular El Porto area, it was Loomis who helped get Obbema his first bouncer's job, at The Garage.

"We used to sit around and have lunch with O.J. (Simpson) and his (first) wife (Marguerite) and their kids," said Loomis, who later spent six years as a U.S. Navy submariner. So Loomis said he also was able to get Simpson's lifelong sidekick and Wild Bunch member, Trojan lineman Cowlings, a bouncing job at The Garage.

The Garage consisted of an actual walled-off garage underneath an office building, with four separate little drinking establishments tucked inside.

In a seemingly very early precursor to such television fare as *Dancing with the Stars, So You Think You Can Dance?* and *Dance Your Ass Off,* The Garage conducted regular dance contests with $100 prizes. Moreover, things could get rougher than mere dancing, Obbema said, since someone once pulled a gun on him there.

"One night, some L.A. cops came in about 1 a.m. when we closed at 2," Loomis said. "They wanted to drink after 1:30, when we stopped serving, and we had to escort them out."

This state of affairs didn't sit well with the constabulary, so Loomis believes revenge was a later motive by some of the spurned off-duty police officers.

What aggravated things even more was some questionable, post-midnight driving in a car full of hungry young drunks – something like "If this is after-hours, it must be Chinese."

"John Smith, (another friend) Bernie Rang and I were at the bar before we took off to go to Chinatown," Obbema recalls. "Bernie had just passed his oral exam for his Ph.D., and we were getting drunk."

"We got shit-faced, no doubt about it," said John G. Smith, who was in the car with Obbema

144

driving, and Rang the other passenger. Before they departed The Garage, Smith said they had to leave behind two larger-than-normal young women who were propping up Loomis. "We piled into the car and got some crazy notion about going to Chinatown" about five miles away "to get some Chinese food."

Obbema was driving and swerving from curb to curb. When police pulled the car over, Rang was throwing up out the window, and had leaned out so far that he fell out of the car, which was going very slowly.

"As we got near downtown," which is just south of Chinatown, "there were red lights behind us, so we pulled over into a vacant lot," Smith said. "As we pull over, Joey's rolling about 2 miles an hour, and Bernie opens the door and reaches up with his hand, and me reaching over trying to pull him back into the car."

The arresting officer informed Obbema that he had run a red light and that he was intoxicated, then handcuffed him, hitting him in the back of the head with his night stick.

"The next thing I know, there's a cop standing there with another cop and, all of a sudden, Joe is down in the backseat of the cop car" with the night-stick-wielding policeman standing ominously over him, Smith said.

"I didn't have a chance after that," Obbema said. "The cop told me to get out of the car and told me to turn around, and I told him I was going to kick his ass. That was a mistake (because) he really knew how to use the stick. I guess that was the only fight I lost," although that claim, while plausible with the tough-fisted Obbema, is certainly not totally verifiable – in many regards.

Obbema wound up in a holding tank at the police station, and Smith talked the cops into letting Smith drive the car home.

Obbema had been detained for a few hours, in the holding area called "The Glass House," charged with the red-light and drunken-driving violations, when all along he insisted he was *not* drunk. Being a strapping, healthy young man capable of losing his temper quickly, especially when he thought in his own mind that he was innocent, Obbema reacted with further rage, once at the lockup.

The now-white-maned Loomis, who today is in his late 60s and a semi-retired stockbroker living on California's Palos Verdes Peninsula, said that when he and Smith arrived at the facility later the same morning, the jailers were beside themselves.

146

"The cops wouldn't go in (the cell) to get him because Joe tore the intercom off the wall," he said. Following several hours' more discussion, Loomis said, they were able to calm down the frustrated young Obbema and get him released.

Loomis said the incident probably stemmed from a perceived "vendetta" that went on for about six months along one stretch of always-busy Wilshire where drunken-driving tickets were being issued in wholesale fashion, especially to anyone even remotely linked to The Garage.

The day in court a couple of weeks later resulted in Obbema appearing wearing his USC varsity jacket. Loomis and Smith helped him get the violation reduced to a "23106," denoting the section of the state motor vehicle code. That meant "driving under the influence of a non-narcotic drug sample: aspirin," accompanied by a minor fine. Yet it did not hurt as well that the judge and prosecuting attorney were both USC School of Law graduates. That Trojan Mystique had worked wonders again.

Justifiable or not, it was a classic example of being in the wrong place at the wrong time, the way Obbema sees it.

The incident had ramifications months later when young Obbema was job-hunting and had been hired by an employer, whom he impressed – up to a point.

For the first six weeks, he was in the top 10 in sales, and "all of a sudden, this manager calls me in and says he has to fire me because I have a drug charge on my record." The dumbfounded Obbema said he contested the technicality but was unable to reverse the dismissal from the job.

With Joe Obbema having finished enough class work to earn his bachelor's degree, he turned his focus toward getting a teaching credential, so that he could teach and coach at the high school level while deciding which direction his life would take him.

He spent a year coaching middle-school sports at the Catholic parish in which he had grown up, St. Pius V, in Buena Park, just across the freeway from the family home on busy Orangethorpe Avenue.

But what turned out to be a further extension of The Wild Bunch, it appeared, was an ostensibly innocuous, part-time job as a bouncer for two years at Cisco's, a pre-sports-bar-era establishment in the

El Porto Beach portion of Manhattan Beach jointly owned by actor Clint Eastwood, singer/comedian Dick Smothers and character actor Jack Ging.

Ging, who grew up in little Alva, Okla., had been a halfback for the Bud Wilkinson-coached Oklahoma Sooners' squad that set an NCAA record 47-game winning streak in the early 1950s, then later co-starred in the popular television series, *The A-Team*, as Gen."Bull" Fullbright. That ownership group had been preceded by Carol Burnett.

Jon Loomis already had plenty of bouncing experience when he convinced the celebrity co-owners of Cisco's to add Obbema to their bouncer contingent.

El Porto was in an unincorporated strip for a long time before eventually being annexed into Manhattan Beach. It had a collection of bars wedged into several blocks between the main drag through the area, Highland Avenue, on the east, and the three or four blocks to the west, between 40th and 45th streets, that separated Highland from what is now Manhattan State Beach and a street/sidewalk called The Strand. El Porto also was popular with surfers, who took advantage of an underground natural phenomenon, which was responsible for producing what board *aficionados* regarded as especially "cherry" waves.

Some believed that the old Standard Oil refinery just up Highland from El Porto caused the unusual semi-seismic activity. (Oil is so plentiful in the nearby vicinity that, next-door in tiny Hermosa Beach, some entrepreneurs were given the OK in 2012 for controversial land-borne drilling just inland from the ocean despite the usual histrionics of rabid environmentalists.)

(Even in the apocalyptic disaster film, *2012*, released before Christmas 2009, one of the small streets in El Porto gets about two minutes of screen time as the asphalt starts to buckle open in some early scenes looking down toward the Pacific Ocean. It may have been that the film's producers already were well aware of the area's shaky past.)

What went on in the few blocks away from the sand and surf, however, consisted of more-unnatural phenomena – on a nightly basis – and that is where Joe Obbema came in.

As he saw it, the ex-USC football player was hired to mind his own business until and unless some rowdies decided to endanger the property or life and limb of otherwise peaceful patrons. Simultaneously, for a period, he also was hired as a bouncer at Torrance's Front Page and Llama Room, smaller "beer bars" where sometimes-renegade bikers had a penchant for causing trouble. His fellow Cisco's bouncers included old roommates Loomis and Smith, plus two guys named Nick Nickles and Arnie Peacock.

Peacock had been a championship boxer in the Army of whom Loomis admits with a retrospective tinge of fear and wariness in his voice, "I never got in a fight with him despite being a bouncer for years." (Torrance and Manhattan Beach are separated from each other by smaller Hermosa Beach.)

"Arnie Peacock was one the three toughest people I ever met," Obbema concurred with Loomis, but not elaborating on exactly whom *the other two* were.

While all this was transpiring, Obbema, teaching certificate in hand, also accepted a part-time coaching job at West High School in Torrance, and additionally nurtured an evolving friendship with another West teacher/coach named Mike Eaton. Eaton was a fellow former Trojan football lineman from the early-to-mid-'60s, who also got Obbema interested in a local rugby club with Loomis.

Obbema shared an apartment with another rugger, Abdulrahim "Abi" Almulla, whom Obbema and Loomis agree was "a dead ringer for Omar

Sharif." At this point, one might ask when Joe Obbema had time to eat and sleep. He did not need to as long as his fists were in good enough shape to "protect the public and preserve property" that was unnecessarily being damaged.

Ron Yary, Obbema's former USC Outland Trophy-winning All-America teammate who already was beginning to fashion a Pro Football Hall of Fame career as a perennial All-Pro offensive tackle with the Minnesota Vikings, said he never cared much for hanging out at such venues. So when he came home from the Twin Cities each off-season, he adeptly steered clear of them.

"I tried to avoid flammable situations," said Yary, who grew up in the nearby inland community of Bellflower. He said it was no use being in a no-win predicament, "even if you were right."

He knows, however, that his friend Joe Obbema was ideally suited to handle his bouncer's job. Yary said that while Obbema has appeared gruff to some, he nevertheless was "affable, approachable and very welcoming when you talk to him . . . always willing to help.

"He always protects the individual from the bully. . . . There were a lot of guys on our team who were that way, but without much anger or purpose to harm," Yary said. "We went right to the edge but knew when to pull back, knew when to stop," he said.

Like Yary, fellow Trojans Bill Hayhoe and Steve Grady were not big on habituating the beach-area clubs, or on taking in the nightlife in general, even though they had been Obbema's college teammates. Ironically, Grady and his wife have lived in Manhattan Beach for years, a little more than a mile from El Porto, yet the beach bars might as well be on another planet, as far as the Gradys are concerned.

"He hung around other people than what I did," Hayhoe said of Obbema. "I didn't hang out much; I had a girlfriend." Hayhoe said on the rare occasions when he frequented the clubs, he would go to a place called The Strand, on its namesake sidewalk/street that fronts the blue Pacific.

"Cisco's was a place to meet and eat and chase women," 70-year-old Mike Eaton said while relaxing at his Las Vegas, Nev., retirement abode. In other words, in the parlance of the Beach Cities that lined the nearby Pacific Coast Highway, or

PCH for short, it was "a beach bar with bitchin' babes."

"He's a very loving, caring person, but don't fuck with him," Eaton said bluntly yet with a straight face regarding Obbema. Eaton, who had stood 6-foot-3 and weighed in at 217 pounds in his Trojan playing days, also had been a sometimes-sparring partner for the Southland's favorite son, the late heavyweight boxing contender Jerry Quarry, so he knew a thing or two himself about fisticuffs and the value of not picking fights.

In fact, as it turns out, Quarry in the flesh occasionally showed up at Cisco's, which no longer exists. But the boxer, blue-collar-Bellflower-bred like RonYary, did not enjoy the surroundings for using his hands; he plied his "pipes," so to speak – Quarry liked to sing at Cisco's, according to reminiscences by someone who posted a blog on the Quarry Foundation website.

> "A wild night at one of the most popular places at the beach, '60s music/dancing and partying . . . and who walked in? The buzz was that Jerry Quarry was in the house," is how a 1969 visit by the professional pugilist

to Cisco's was characterized in a 1999 blog by someone identified only as Robert.

"He was not only at Cisco's, but could *sing* and did, and took in the revelry of the night. A most engaging night for me and rest of my friends," wrote Robert, who in the blog went on to emphasize that he (Robert), who was born in the same year as Quarry in 1945, later was involved in the Space Shuttle program, launching others into orbit in a different way than the heavyweight boxer did in the ring.

Blogger Robert stated on the Quarry Foundation website that the older of his two daughters (age 21 at the time of the '99 blog-site entry) attended "a local university and lives only minutes from where Cisco's once existed. We recently shared lunch together just down the street, as I reminisced of earlier times here. However, it doesn't change that moment in time, a fond memory of that night at Cisco's . . . and Manhattan Beach."

Cisco's was born as a companion club to a Mexican restaurant called Pancho's – named after the charming pair of *Don Quixote/Sancho Panza* types originally created by short-story author O. Henry. The pair of *caballeros* became even more popular in a 1950s television series, *The Cisco Kid.* While Pancho's remained at the original site, Cisco's moved across Highland Avenue to its own locale; Cisco's, under numerous ownership changes, has progressively been named Harry O's and OB's.

Apparently, unlike the old Julie's Restaurant that once stood near the USC campus, Cisco's/Harry O's/OB's has no sandwich or other food item named after Joe Obbema, despite his years of service protecting the surroundings with his fists.

"I never saw Joe start anything. He always tried to negotiate with guys first," Eaton, a 40-year teaching and coaching veteran, said of the Cisco's bouncer Obbema. "Joe would've been a perfect candidate for Ultimate Fighting" if that activity had been available in those days. Put more succinctly, Obbema didn't typically start fights but he always seemed to finish them, usually on the winning end (the L.A. cop with the night stick being a stark exception).

Obbema said the multiple celebrity partners made it clear to him from the outset precisely what his mission would be.

He accompanied Peacock into Cisco's office to meet with the three celebrity owners, and had orders to toss unruly bikers who were part of a gang headed by a big biker named Lobo. Lobo was about 6-feet tall, bald, with an out-of-joint nose, and covered with tattoos – in a bygone era when only rough, shady guys, sailors or Marines had "tats." Rumors had abounded all along the beach that the bad bikers were coming to break up the place. Eastwood told Obbema and Peacock, "We're tired of having bikers in here; it's bad for business." Then Obbema asked, "Well, Clint, what do you want us to do?" And Eastwood replied, in characteristic Dirty Harry fashion, "Don't kill nobody."

"So for three weeks we were throwing bikers out of the bar — throw 'em out, throw 'em out, throw 'em out," Obbema said.

The following Friday night before the biker group's expected Sunday arrival, someone described by Obbema as "one of the largest human beings I'd ever seen" walked into Cisco's. His name was Bobby Menter, and he was a professional wrestler and reputedly a cousin of Hulk Hogan. Menter, apparently a decent-enough guy but only to a point, was hired to help him to combat the expected invasion of bikers, who always parked (illegally) in the red zone on the street out front.

"He was a pretty big guy; you wanted to get to know him pretty good and find out what his intentions were. You didn't want to fight *against* him," Obbema said. In other words, he said that while Menter "was a really nice guy who had been injured wrestling," once the Hogan relative went into action, you definitely wanted him on *your* side.

Obbema took Menter aside and, confiding that a big problem was anticipated for Sunday, informed him that about seven or eight bikers were planning to come in and create havoc for a day or two. After the bikers' arrival about mid-afternoon that Sunday, Obbema and Menter tried to stress as diplomatically as possible that the motorcycles had to be removed from the red zone, which precipitated a brawl. Accompanying Obbema and Menter in that Sunday's bouncer cadre were Nickles and Obbema's old roommate, Loomis. (To this day, there are those few cynics who might dispute this account – or that bikers even frequented Cisco's -- yet there also exists more-than-enough evidence to counter that cynicism.)

According to Obbema, after the fair warning, Lobo informed him, "We didn't come down here to drink; we just came down here to kick your . . .," at which point the bouncer let him have it with a brisk right jab, Obbema's stock-in-trade punch.

Bottom line, after the smoke cleared and the bodies had flown: The bouncers won, despite being outnumbered at least 2-to-1.

"We stacked eight bikers in criss-cross fashion on the sidewalk in the front," Obbema said. The police showed up, and Obbema hinted that the offenders needed to be put in jail. Then the police sergeant looked over at them and said with a smile, "Hell, Joe, they might want to put *you* in jail."

After the bikers were jailed, they sued Obbema for assault and battery. "The bikers' attorney got up in court to tell how *I* 'attacked' eight bikers, -- and these guys were big human beings," Obbema said, stretching his arm straight over his head to emphasize *how* big. The bikers' lawyer "got about two or three sentences out of his mouth, when the judge stopped him and asked, 'Wait a minute, you telling me that Mr. Obbema, an educated man, getting his credential, attacked these bikers?' Then the judge looked down and said, 'Case dismissed. Get outta here. This is ridiculous.'

"What was really neat about those days, when you won, things were over. Now they might come back and shoot you," Obbema said. "This couldn't happen now, but back then, we had a lot looser situation."

Loomis and Smith relish their own personal remembrances of the bouncer scene at Cisco's, even though they did not always have regular contact with the co-owners.

Eastwood tried to pick up Loomis's fiancée, and Loomis warned him, treading dangerously, considering Eastwood was one of his bosses.

Another time, a prospective patron got off his motorcycle and tried to cut in line in front of maybe 50 people with a younger-looking date.

Said Loomis, "He started yelling at me because I said, 'You look like you're 21, but your girlfriend looks like she's 14.' Then Jack Ging put his hand on my shoulder and instructed me to let him in. I asked, "why?' and Ging said, 'Because he owns the place'."

The line-cutter, it turns out, was Dick Smothers.

In the bouncing job Obbema had at Torrance's Front Page while coaching and student-teaching at nearby West High, a group of four biker types apparently had revenge on their minds for having been "bounced" previously from the establishment. Since the club was merely a "beer bar," as opposed to a "whiskey" bar, he said it tended to attract more bikers.

Apparently, the four became angry and vowed to return soon. Therefore, Obbema told the owner to expect a fight, and when the owner asked how he knew, Obbema said that is what he was being paid for. When the four showed up, there were two guys in the front and two in back, with Obbema informing them they could not enter.

"This was in the early '70s. I had just kind of driven up when it was starting," Eaton remembers. "Joe hit about two guys and they went down like timber, and the other two guys kind of backed away. Joe had very quick hands."

"I know enough about bouncing in a bar; I wasn't going to try and talk these guys out of it; it wasn't going to work. So, I told 'em one time to leave, and the guy started to hit me, and I hit him, and the back of his head hit the other guy, and knocked them both out," Obbema said. "Then the other guy took a swing at me with a pipe, and he missed me, hit me in the shoulder. And then I hit this guy, and knocked him out, and there's this one guy standing there."

In Obbema's mind, the action lasted only 15 seconds. He asked the last standing biker what he wanted to do, and the biker meekly murmured, "nothing," then mounted his bike and rode off quickly. The remaining, unconscious violator was hauled off to jail when the police arrived.

The only differentiation in versions between Obbema and Eaton was in the number of mere seconds it took to dispatch the troublemakers.

Obbema said that Eaton and another coach who witnessed the fracas "couldn't believe it happened that quickly." Eaton thought it took 30 seconds, but when it is a matter of a blink of a couple eyelashes between friends, who cares anyway?

Then there was the time in the Llama Room, a separate cocktail lounge in the same building as the Front Page.

A drunken Asian bar patron decided to "remodel" the bathroom by trying to tear out the sink.

"This Asian guy was busting up the bathroom and Joe went in and said 'Get your ass outta here' and put his lights out," Eaton said. Eaton was sitting in the front of the bar on a brick planter when the Asian man came around from the back of the bar.

"Mike was really a kind guy and, after he saw how hurt this guy was, he went over to see if he could help," Obbema said. Obbema then yelled at Eaton to inform him this was the guy who the former had just thrown out and who had spat upon him.

Realizing this, Eaton punched the Asian in the face, knocking him back severely.

"Can you imagine how that guy must have felt the next day?" Obbema said.

Eaton said he was maybe 29 to 30 years old at the time, and Obbema about 5-6 years younger.

There was yet another bit of unintended hilarity that happened during Obbema's time at Cisco's. The Southern rock group Black Oak Arkansas was playing, and ex-roomie John G. Smith also was doing a bouncing turn.

"If their lead guitarist (Michael "Narley Dude" Martin) hadn't (overdosed and died years later), they would've been a really good band," Obbema asserted with the same kind of certainty with which he went about life in general. "They came in to play. We were charging $5 a door to get in."

"There were always long lines around the corner" at Cisco's, "to see really good bands," Loomis said.

"The last thing you want to do is have a fight in the bar with all these people in it," Obbema said. At any rate, while Black Oak was in the middle of its gig, Obbema said that "there was guy in there in about his 40s – most of the guys in there were about 21 to 30 years old – and so the guy was drinking and messing with girls. He was only about 5-9, maybe 160 pounds, so I took him out back and had to tell him, 'I don't want to hurt you, and you don't want me to hurt you.'"

The older guest then spat on Obbema, who grabbed him by the hair to punch him in the face, when, to Obbema's amazement, he pulled off his full toupee. As the instantly "hairless" man took off running down the street, Obbema yelled out, "Oh, my God, I think I scalped him!"

Smith was laughing so hard that he almost fell down the stairs.

At the break, Obbema walked up to the owners' table, where Eastwood, Ging and Smothers were. Obbema tossed the toupee on the table, making Eastwood "almost jump out of his skin." One of the co-owners then proclaimed, "Jesus Christ, what the hell is that?"

After closing time, the co-owners and their bouncer stayed around until about 5 a.m., laughing over the episode. By the way, the owner of the toupee never returned to reclaim it.

About two weeks later, Obbema was standing at the back of the bar next to some Dutch doors, with the top door open but the bottom door locked.

A burly guy somewhat similar in size to Obbema – about, 6-2 and 225 pounds – started to walk out of the back with a drink, being told by Obbema that the latter worked there and that the law would not allow the former to take the drink out of the bar.

The patron responded by hitting the bouncer with the glass, to which Obbema returned the favor by bopping him back and knocking him into an upright position between the cigarette machine and the wall. Obbema hit him a couple more times before being grabbed by a bartender named John Jackson who urged him to stop.

Then another bouncer, Nick Nickles, grabbed the offender's friend so they could eject them from the club, at which point, the friend swung at Obbema, who swung back, causing the friend to career into the street. The bouncers took the original offender and put him on the sidewalk, quickly locking the Dutch door.

"When I said to Nick, 'Shouldn't we get that guy out of the street?' " Obbema said. "He answered, 'It's OK, Joe, he's in the crosswalk.' "

Obbema did not have much daily interaction with the three celebrity partners who were his official bosses at Cisco's.

Yet he remembers he and golfing buddy Gene Alexander bumping into Cisco's regular Lee Majors, "The Six Million Dollar Man," at an all-star golf event years later. When the Bionic Man saw him, Majors said, "You look familiar." Obbema said, "You look like Lee Majors" and he said, "You look like Joe Obbema." Then the TV star simply declared, "How the hell are you?" -- as if to give tribute to the big bouncer, from the place Majors had frequented, who tried to keep the peace in his own unique way – without any bionic help. Majors, now in his 70s, has been seen in recent years on a television informercial in late-night TV spots

166

hawking a snazzy, new hearing device to which he had lent his name.

Mike Eaton will always reckon that his buddy the bouncer left one trademark, though.

"The best weapon he had was the ('67) national championship ring. There (were) a lotta guys running around this town with 'national champion' (etched) on their face," Eaton said with a knowing grin. This is a very likely explanation since Obbema always led with lightning-fast quickness with his right – the same hand that holds the championship ring finger.

After which came rugby and all the attendant doings, including the extra job of driving a beer truck on the West Hollywood route.

"I taught and coached at Paramount High School for two years before going down to West Torrance," Obbema said, emphasizing that the comparative demographics were like the difference between night and day. Even though the center of Paramount is only about 12 street miles from its Torrance equivalent, the contrast between the two communities is more like one measured in light-years, it seems. "I just wanted to go back, get my degree, and teach and coach football."

For the record, Paramount, a smaller, older community not too far southeast of downtown Los Angeles, is largely Hispanic (72 percent) with a population of about 55,000, according to government statistics. The per-capita family income is $37,000. Its most notable claim to fame is as the birthplace and still-home of the Zamboni, the machine that shaves the ice at hockey games all over the world.

Torrance, by contrast, has nearly three times the population at 149,000, 59 percent of it white, with an $85,000 per-capita family income. It is about 30 miles due south of downtown Los Angeles, and close to the Pacific Ocean with a small shoreline of its own pinched in between Redondo Beach on the north and Palos Verdes Estates to the south at the end of a short street named Vista del Mar. Torrance enjoys a healthier economic base than Paramount as the U.S. headquarters of two major Japanese carmakers, Toyota and Honda, and also is home to one of the nation's older mega-shopping malls, Del Amo Fashion Center, shooting locale for some of local-boy director Quentin Tarantino's film projects.

Eaton said his early teaching and coaching experience had been similar to Obbema's. He logged his first two years at a junior high school in low-income Watts, site of the massive 1965 riots, before spending the remainder of his 40-year career at West Torrance.

"When I took over at Paramount – I was defensive coordinator – they hadn't won a game in five years. They actually were the worst football team I'd ever seen in my life," Obbema said. "I coached there another year, and they turned the program around. When they finally won a game, the whole town went berserk."

Once he arrived in Torrance, Obbema said, "I was fortunate enough . . . my best friend was Mike Eaton," with whom he hooked up as a fellow assistant football coach at West High for two more years. Then it was not too long before Obbema was introduced by Eaton and Abi Almulla to the nuances of rugby. They even had a genuine South African coach named Graham K. Eddy, not unlike what was depicted by actor Matt Damon in the 2011 Oscar-nominated movie, *Invictus*.

Rugby has been described as a "hooligans' sport played by gentlemen," as compared to soccer, which has been regarded as "a gentlemen's sport played by hooligans." (Apologies to soccer *aficionados*). As the dual-bouncer's jobs continued, Obbema found kinship among his fellow ruggers. Being one of the bigger, taller members of his club, he assumed the role as an "outsider," a position similar to football's running-back designation.

"Joe was bouncing at Cisco's" when the rugby bug first bit, Eaton said. Since his roommate and best new coaching friend already were immersed with the rugby club, it was only natural for Obbema to enjoy his adopted sport.

Although Obbema and former Trojan teammate Fred Khasigian were quite different – in general tastes, personalities and usually with whom they normally hung around – each loved movies. Therefore, they occasionally used that affinity to confound rugby opponents.

"Fred was a very intelligent man, almost introverted," the loquacious Obbema said. "Right in front of the other team, we pretended he was Rod Steiger and I was Marlon Brando, as we re-enacted a famous scene from *On the Waterfront*, the one where the mob boss is talking to his brother, a longshoreman/boxer. "Rod Steiger said, 'It wasn't your night, that night.'"

So right in the middle of a common rugby procedure known as a lineout, Khasigian would say, "It wasn't your night, that night, kid," to which Obbema would reply, "I would have been a contender; I could have been somebody, but my own brother gave me a one-way ticket to Palooka-ville." Members of the opposing side became confused, wondering what was going on, and thinking Obbema and Khasigian were crazy. The pair used the ploy to their advantage to gain ball possession.

In rugby, it is illegal to use one's elbows to gain an unfair advantage and, in one instance, one of Obbema's four artificial front teeth had been knocked out by an Argentine ruffian by that method. Therefore, Obbema took out one of the dislodged false teeth and handed it to the Argentine coach.

Obbema resumed playing and, on a play-in of the ball straight up the middle, he proceeded to break an opponent's jaw, broke his nose and knocked out two of another player's teeth with a forearm as a return gesture for the loosened false tooth.

"He came to the party later with his jaw wired and he said in Spanish, 'Nice hit!' He had to sip his beer through a straw," Obbema said, laughing lustily at the absurdity of it all.

Then there was the big rugby tournament in Santa Barbara, the first for Obbema and teammates, and also the world's largest of its kind. They were staying in a local college dormitory at Easter break, and after registering, they overheard some potential opponents discussing a big running back from Cisco's. Since Cisco's was in Division II, and the other club in Division I, they did not specifically know Obbema, but it was obvious that *he* was their main topic.

"They couldn't run at me, but they were talking about how they were gonna screw me up in the game, kick my ass, all that stuff," he said.

The next morning, when they were on the field ready to scrum, "the guy who was the biggest loudmouth was the guy who was marking me, the guy (who) was opposite me," Obbema said. "I said 'hi', and the guy turned white. Later on in the game, I got the ball and I hit the guy so hard, he was rolling over backwards as fast as I was running." The referee told Obbema that was the hardest hit he had ever seen. "Playing rugby was a lot more fun than playing football," said Obbema, who also numbered former Mater Dei and USC teammate Steve Pultorak as a later rugby teammate.

Eaton soon found out about his coaching consort's taste, or distaste, for a certain popular sandwich adornment or salad staple – something that has been described varyingly as a vegetable or fruit, but not known as a missile until in the hands of an angry Joseph Obbema.

"This was like Friday night. Joe didn't get off 'til about 2 or 3 a.m., and I picked him up," Eaton said. "We stopped for breakfast at a place in Oceanside on the way to an 8 a.m. start in San Diego" for a rugby tournament.

That is when Eaton learned that Obbema hates tomatoes.

"It was a tiny restaurant and he didn't want breakfast; he wanted a burger," Eaton said. "We sat at a counter and two CHP (California Highway Patrol) officers sat in a booth right behind us. Joe opened the burger and found a tomato, then spun around and threw it. It stuck to the window right by the two cops. Joe said, 'I told the waitress I didn't want a tomato,' then the two cops got up and walked out without saying anything."

Postscript admission by Obbema: "It's true. I really *do* hate tomatoes."

Which leads one to wonder further about the Joe Obbema namesake chicken sandwich that was on the menu at Julie's Restaurant: Did it, or did it not, include tomatoes?

Back out on the rugby field itself, other things were happening.

"We used to play this team that was mostly Tongans and some Samoans," Eaton related. "One Samoan named Toughie was huge. When he held a pitcher, it looked like a cup in his hands. Joe and I wound up opposite of this guy and we wound up directly doubling him. My head wound up in his tummy and Joe's head in his chest. He was so big that we looked like two Ping-Pong balls."

The brand of rugby played by the Torrance club was exactly *that*: Club rugby.

"It's more to have fun," Eaton said, "except the Santa Monica team ruined the whole thing. For us, practice was an excuse to go drink beer."

While all this bouncing and rugging and chugging and . . . was going on, the two coaches/ruggers found time for yet another pastime – in which it in one instance resembled the dart games in the pubs where Obbema worked.

"We were building furniture. Joe was making these tables out of kiln-dried redwood. Joe's craftsmanship and my idea . . . were a little different. I got pissed off one time and threw a screwdriver, which wound up in the wall," much to Obbema's consternation, Eaton said. Despite his predilection for the drink, Eaton would want anybody to know that the screwdriver he tossed was the traditional tool type.

Obbema still had a bit of bouncer in him, so to speak, nearly two decades ago, when he let temper get the better of him in the Coliseum parking lot after a disappointing loss to intersectional archrival Notre Dame – with good buddy and longtime Trojan booster Ed Posthuma the target.

"At that time, you were able to park right in front of the Coliseum, where the statues are," said the 6-foot-7 Posthuma. "Right after the game in the parking lot, my wife and I beat them back to our van. Joe came flying back, with my side sliding door open, and tackled me. He was so pissed off he just dove at me, hit me, and knocked me down. It wasn't too funny."

Throughout the ensuing three-plus decades of a successful sales career, an avocation as a sports photographer, and that constant keeping an eye out for others, Joe Obbema faced one tragic circumstance after another – punctuated nonetheless by his own personal triumphs and continued survival. They were events that were born not only out of the Wild Bunch but even further back during Obbema's formative football days in the Orange County youth leagues and later at Mater Dei High School.

6

TRAGEDY, TRIUMPH AND TRANSITION

Show me a hero and I will write you a tragedy.

-- Notebooks, F. Scott Fitzgerald (1896-1940)

Hall of Fame offensive tackle Ron Yary is a no-nonsense type of guy. Throughout his life – from all the years he played football in high school, college and the National Football League, and carrying over to his career as a commercial real estate professional – he has subscribed to a single credo: Pay attention to the task at hand.

"The offensive line – you have to be attentive to the game and the action," Yary said. "It requires intelligence."

Asked if he thought there was a correlation between what happens on a football field and in combat in the military – even though he never was in the latter – the 1967 Outland and Walter Camp award winner from the University of Southern California surmised that there is indeed a connection.

Like genuine combat – the kind with bullets and grenades – Yary said that gridiron participants are involved in a struggle that develops an ultimate bond, which often lasts a lifetime.

"Football is the only sport I know of that creates the sentiment" that one experiences on the military battlefield, he said. "You're in a struggle . . . It's the same thing in football with the heightening of emotion. The adrenaline and other hormones are pumping at a maximum level."

Yary, now age 67, played 15 seasons in the NFL, all but one of those seasons with Minnesota, but blossomed big-time as the top collegiate lineman in the nation, blocking in his senior year for fellow College and Pro Football Hall of Famer O.J. Simpson.

Pondering the question whether he made Simpson better or vice-versa, Yary replied, "A little bit of both."

When a talented offensive lineman has a tailback like Simpson operating behind him, Yary said that "it always gives you hope and the expectation (success will) occur, so you never let up . . . out of respect for him."

While the perennial All-Pro tackle enjoyed being a "yin" to Simpson's "yang," he likewise draws no distinction between a big star such as Simpson and the other players on the USC Trojan team that was consensus National Champion in 1967.

One of those others was defensive end Joe Obbema, two years younger than Yary but tough as nails, in the latter's book. The mutual respect and admiration between the two was so strong that it has carried over to this day in real life.

"You have to admire that more, standing on the sidelines in the cold and getting stiff," Yary said of Obbema and the other Trojans who were either reserves or who manned special teams (kickoffs, punts and field-goal and extra-point attempts).

The abiding relationship between the two today is such that either can pick up the phone on speed-dial and chat with the other about almost anything, even though Yary resides in Southern California and Obbema several years ago moved from Nevada to Texas.

"That's why they call it a team sport," Yary said of that binding element football creates despite the two parties having gone in decidedly different directions since they were college teammates.

"(Obbema) was always a wide-eyed guy on the sidelines, always pleased to be part of the Trojan Mystique," said Chuck Dekeado, who worked in an advisory role for 15 years for the late USC Head Coach John McKay, who led the '67 squad.

"He is one of those kind of guys who'd always come through, on the field, or off," 97-year-old Nick Pappas said of Obbema. The seemingly ageless Pappas, who lives with his daughter, Mona, in Pasadena, Calif., is a USC legend; since the 1930s, he has been a Trojan football player, assistant coach and associate athletic director. In 1997, Pappas was inducted into the USC Athletic Hall of Fame. Pappas is deservedly known to all in the Trojan Family as "Mr. Trojan."

For Joe Obbema, after he earned his teaching certificate and balanced multiple jobs as a bouncer in Southland beach-city bars while coaching part-time at Paramount and West Torrance high schools, many of the next 35 years were spent as a successful sales manager and representative in the transportation industry.

Obbema said he procured his bachelor's degree in marketing because "I always wanted to go into the marketing field, into marketing products. I knew I was a good salesperson."

During those same years, he encountered life's bumps and bruises – taking a shot at this, getting knocked down by that, yet pulling himself up each time a tad stronger. It lent credence to those who, over time, had more than just casually suggested that he would have made a decent prizefighter.

Wherever he went, and whatever he tried to accomplish, Obbema always engendered respect from those who knew him best – close friends and family – as they watched him time after time helping those less fortunate.

During Obbema's long career in the trucking and transportation business, he had some unusual requests.

For instance, there was a Boston-born client in Southern California "who wanted to be buried in his native soil," Obbema said. "So he wanted 12 pounds of dirt shipped out." But when you ship LTL – or less-than-truckload – there never has been a specific classification for dirt. Therefore, Obbema called a competitor who was a veteran of the business and "he knew the class of dirt was 77½," and the soil was shipped from coast to coast to enable the Massachusetts native to have his unusual request granted.

Obbema's two offspring from the 12-year marriage to his first wife were a good example of his selflessness, as he was awarded custody of them resulting from her serious eating disorder. The youngsters eventually combined with various step- or adopted siblings to form a blended family that included a total of seven children who today have reached various junctures of adulthood.

"She unfortunately had contracted anorexia. I actually went bankrupt trying to get her well. It was taking a very bad emotional toll on my children," he said. "I was giving her $500" a month for child support. But the judge looked at me and said, 'I don't know who your lawyer was, but *she* should be paying you' . . . And the entire courtroom exploded into laughter."

Obbema said his first wife lost so much weight that she dropped as low as 68 pounds and, even though he was able to get her back into a treatment center, she unfortunately reverted to the same disorder in less than a month.

One of the couple's close friends, in fact, anonymously said, "She got to the point where she kept telling me how fat she thought she was, and she was down to 80 pounds at that point. I guess that's one of the big dangers of a disease like that."

While still married to his first wife, Obbema always worked two, sometimes even three, jobs. It was not uncommon, for several years, for him to work continuously from 5:30 a.m. to 11 p.m. daily.

While he was raising his two biological children – a son and daughter – after the mid-1980s divorce, Obbema simultaneously branched out into a long-term sidelight in addition to sales: Sports photography, which had begun merely as a hobby.

"We would go to Little League parks, Pop Warner, places like that, and we got pretty good at it," he said of the shutterbug sidelight.

As he got better, in his rounds with a still camera, Obbema would develop a friendship with Dick "Night Train" Lane, official photographer of the Detroit Lions who died in 2002 at age 74. The irony of those encounters was that Lane, who also was with the Los Angeles Rams and St. Louis Cardinals, closed out his career as a defensive back with the Lions from 1960-65 and set an NFL single-season record with 14 interceptions. The Lions, of course -- through Lane's old teammate Jim Martin -- were the only NFL team that had offered a younger Obbema a chance for a tryout.

Showing up at different sports events with his camera bag tethered onto one shoulder, Obbema often surprised old friends and acquaintances alike.

"I remember a night game with the San Diego Chargers when Joe came up with his camera and I turned around and I said, 'Hi, Joe'," said Dave Levy, by then in the 1980s a Chargers assistant coach. The surprised Levy was an assistant during Obbema's USC playing days and had not seen him for several years despite having collaborated with him a time or two on charity events, so he gladly complied with any of the budding camera guy's photo requests.

Chuck Dekeado, John McKay's unofficial USC recruiting coordinator, said that he had watched Obbema since Mater Dei High and in college but that the latter became really good with the camera two decades later when Dekeado was marketing director for a budding pro-football enterprise.

"I bumped into him 20 years later. I was with the (USFL's Los Angeles) Express, who Joe did the collage for," said Dekeado, now 76 and living in Henderson, Nev., outside Las Vegas. "He was a hell of a photographer."

During the period when Joe Obbema was separated from his first wife – and working for Consolidated Freightways – he met another woman, named Maureen, but whom everyone affectionately called "Mo." Mo was in the process of getting a divorce; she was a fun-loving person with two children, also a girl and a boy, who were older than Obbema's offspring.

"We planned on getting married after our divorces were over with," Obbema said. "Our involvement had nothing to do with the break-up of our former marriages."

The stress of a tough job and having two kids of his own at home had taken a terrible toll on Obbema's health. Beverly, Mo's daughter and older of her two children, was getting married, and her prospective stepfather volunteered to pay for the wedding – a characteristically charitable gesture by the big-hearted former Trojan player. During the ceremony, however, Obbema experienced chest pains, yet he only confided in his younger brother, Bob, about it, because Joe Obbema did not want anyone else to worry. The next day, Bob insisted his older brother go to the hospital – which was good advice, since the older Obbema had a heart attack at the hospital.

A USC team doctor and a friend of Obbema's, Dr. Francis, told the former Trojan player that he needed an angioplasty to unclog three arteries. The day after the procedure, Mo visited her fiancé in the hospital, and she was supposed to return the following day but never showed.

"I got really worried and called my mom to see if she had heard from her," Obbema said. "She told me Mo was supposed to be there at the hospital, and I just had this feeling that something was wrong."

So Obbema called down to the emergency room of the same hospital where he was recovering, and he was informed by a nurse that Mo had been admitted because of a brain hemorrhage and was in very bad condition. When the nurse realized she was talking to Mo's future husband who was a patient himself, she instructed him to remain in his room, and told him there was nothing he could do.

Instead of staying put, the naturally impulsive and stubborn Obbema ripped the intravenous tubes from his arm and dashed toward the elevators. Fortunately, his doctor was in the hospital and intercepted Obbema. The doctor explained that he could not see his fiancée and detailed to Obbema what had occurred: That Mo had irreversible brain damage and could not live without a respirator.

"On the day I was released from the hospital, Mo's children and I had to make the decision to unplug her from the machines and let her go," Obbema said, regarding the dire decision that happened just six weeks before their scheduled nuptials.

Obbema's sister, Mary Trask, the second of five Obbema children and two years younger than Joe, said that "they found Mo in a bathroom; she had had a stroke and they took her to the hospital. She had passed out a few days earlier at a Wal-Mart, and nothing was wrong then."

Mary said that both Mo's and Joe's families had a faint glimmer of hope when they saw her blink.

"We thought she was OK, but it wasn't so," the elder of two Obbema sisters said of Mo's death soon thereafter.

Said Joe Obbema, "Now I had three kids at home and was a single parent and alone again." He had added Mo's son, Eric Bessette, to his brood as if Eric were his blood relative – no strings attached, again in typically compassionate Obbema fashion. Obbema said that his own aging mother, reflecting on the situation later, had told him that "they don't screw people up this much in soap operas, because it's too mean."

If there is redemption in life, it was afforded by, and to, Obbema's USC teammate, defensive back Sandy Durko. In a 1968 win against Oregon State, Durko, with good intentions, had aggressively dived into a pile and aggravated Obbema's already sore back.

Durko and another '67 Trojan player, Kendall "Butch" Nungesser, were principals in the group that owned massive Rose Hills Memorial Park, near Durko's West Covina home in the San Gabriel Valley. (At the time, Rose Hills was second in size among private cemetery/mausoleums to the more well-known Forest Lawn, the so-called "Final Resting Place of the Stars," only 13 miles to the northwest.)

"I called Sandy, and he said, 'Don't worry about a thing, Joe.' It was very emotional, very hard on me and my kids," Obbema said. He said his children had definitely developed a great affinity for their stepmother-to-be. "A friend, Dick Mitchell, had loaned me the money to pay for it, and Sandy set up the arrangements for a two-person burial plot and coffin at cost.

"We had a good service. A lot of people came. I was kind of in a daze at the time, but I got a lot of things done," Obbema admitted. "We had party, a wake – that's what Maureen would've wanted. The wake was just outstanding."

But Obbema also insisted that Durko offered the service simply "because he was a good guy," nothing more.

Before leaving West Torrance to tackle such multiple jobs as the photography business and even delivering beer in the West Hollywood area, Obbema had coached his youngest brother, Rick, 10 years his junior. Rick had transferred from Buena Park High to be under his brother's tutelage at West Torrance. As one of the most highly sought-after high-school running backs in the nation his senior year, and possessing good speed on a 6-foot-4, 235-pound frame, he advanced to play college football, first at UCLA, and finally at the University of Hawaii, having shifted to linebacker.

But less than two years after Mo's death, a similar fate struck Obbema's other brother, Bob, who was seven years younger than Joe – age 33 at the time. In a two-car accident in the Mojave Desert, Bob Obbema had been riding in the middle of a three-passenger pickup-truck cab. The other vehicle had pushed the truck into a gully upon impact, and Bob Obbema hit his head on a cinder block, killing him instantly.

Since Joe Obbema was listed as next-of-kin, the Riverside County coroner called him. "I told him, 'No, that's impossible. Bobby can't be dead. Then I called Ricky, and he went berserk," Obbema said. "I hadn't smoked in years, but I picked up a pack of cigarettes belonging to my sister Michele's roommate, who was a cocktail waitress, off a table and smoked 'em."

Joe Obbema then went to his parents' house the next day and "stole" his father's cigarettes. He sat in an almost-catatonic state for nearly three hours, smoking one cigarette after another, before he could muster the courage to inform his parents of Bobby's death.

"My mom's doctor, Dr. Wong, he was a really good guy. He was there and he gave her a sedative after I broke the news. He said, "Charline, just relax, I've got something to tell you'," Obbema said. "It was horrible. . . . I can't imagine having one of my children dying before I do." Obbema said he's had his share of scares with his own kids. Daughter Mary Jo suffered a serious bout with pneumonia as a toddler, and there was son Matt's testicular cancer much later.

Not unexpectedly in a family so close, Mary's reaction was much the same as Joe's, she admitted, as was that of younger sister, Michele. Michele, 31 at the time, was closest in both age and spirit to Bob. Their three other siblings admit that Michele and Bob were the two best athletes in a sports-minded family.

"I went ballistic; I was screaming," Mary said. The death of her slightly younger brother "really affected me," Michele, known to her siblings more familiarly as Shelly, said in an interview before she died of congestive heart failure in January 2012 at age 56.

Following a funeral Mass at the Obbemas' old home parish, St. Pius V, in Buena Park (also the site of Shelly's funeral Mass 25 years later), Durko came through again; the USC teammate, who also spent four years playing for the NFL's Cincinnati Bengals and New England Patriots, repeated his generous gesture of two years previous for his Trojan defensive buddy.

Again, Obbema was certain Durko offered the second service for the same simple reason he had done it in the first instance – Sandy Durko was merely a good guy helping a longtime friend and former teammate. It was something that, given the same circumstance but with the roles reversed, Obbema, the tough guy with the enormous heart, surely would have done for Durko, to which some of their former USC teammates would readily attest.

The aforementioned bond among USC athletes in years far beyond their playing days had surfaced once more amid the passing of two people so close to Joe Obbema.

"After Maureen died, the guy who helped me the most was Mike Garrett, who had lost *his* fiancée, too. He called me, and we talked a long time," he said. "Our relationship dated back to SC when I was a freshman to help recruit high school seniors," Obbema said of Garrett, who was longtime USC athletic director until August 2010. Garrett won the Heisman Trophy in 1965 as O.J. Simpson's star predecessor at tailback.

Another friend who helped was former USC and Mater Dei quarterback Toby Page. Unbeknownst to Obbema until then, Page's wife had died prematurely, at the same age 39 as Mo, so the former high school and college teammates shared feelings about the helplessness and pain that accompanies loss of a loved one. (Page, two years older than Obbema, had been the quarterback in the Trojans' 21-20 victory over crosstown rival UCLA to sew up the 1967 consensus national title that earned championship rings for both.)

"It's life more than anything else; it just happens. You have to go on with your life," conceded Page, now in his mid-60s and a longtime stockbroker who still lives in Southern California.

Certainly, Obbema, during this prolonged period of receiving consolation and assistance from others, was not short himself on giving back to others – as has always been customary for him.

"Joe always has had a big heart," former USC teammate Dick Allmon said, likening Obbema to another Trojan squad member, Steve McConnell. McConnell earned a Ph.D. in Sociology and a B.A. from USC. In June 2008, after many years with the non-profit Alzheimer's Association in Washington, D.C., he was named vice president for advocacy and public policy for the Atlantic Philanthropies Ageing Program, also based in the nation's capital.

"You know your teammates. I was there for a bunch of years, and he was there for a bunch of years," Allmon said of someone like Obbema, underscoring the value of that massive Trojan Family network, which has burgeoned over time.

The same networking to which Allmon referred manifested itself well from October 1990 to September 2000. That's when Obbema was the catalyst for organizing an annual charity golf tournament, for 10 years in Orange County, then the final year in Las Vegas, after he and second wife Linda had moved to the gaming capital. The tournament benefited foster children through the S.A.F.E. program, or Southern Area Foster Care Effort, and Obbema made maximum use of his sports and celebrity contacts to attract an interesting annual field of entrants, thus ensuring success. The tournament raised an average of more than $20,000 for foster children's benefit every year.

The late Barbara Labitsky, who died in December 2001, ran the tournament, handling all the logistics. Obbema, who conceded he could not have managed without her, also enlisted a businessman named Scott Crane to be "my right-hand man" for the annual event. The three, each with his or her own special personality and set of talents, proved to be an unbeatable team throughout the '90s.

"Joe liked getting up in front of everybody; I'm just the opposite," said the 50-year-old Crane, who lives in La Palma, Calif. Regardless, Crane said, "it was just about the kids" in either case. He admitted that "I did the dirty work; I went to the golf course earlier and ensured that everything was set up." The tournament's public face, Obbema, concurrently went about the "schmoozing," persuading various celebrities to donate their time for a worthy cause and have some fun along the way.

Crane recalls vividly the day Obbema sealed the deal for them to partner in the charity effort. In fact, the former has a keen mental recollection of that exact moment that occurred at the pipe-fitting manufacturing company of which Crane is part-owner.

"I have a picture in my mind when he was sitting across my desk from me and convinced me to do it," Crane said. "When I met Barbara, I already had heard the story of the (foster) kid with 14 staples in his head." The child who had been abused thusly was one of many foster wards whose plight had attracted the trio of Labitsky, Crane and Obbema into helping such children.

Labitsky, a 60-something woman who was totally dedicated to foster children, originally had helped set up a non-profit for those youths in Orange County called the Orangewood Home, Crane said. Starting with the 12th annual version, the tournament was merged into the Doug DeCinces Orangewood Tournament, with the longtime Baltimore Orioles and California Angels infielder as title host.

While still teaming on the tourney with Obbema and Labitsky, Crane worked out an arrangement for health-insurance company PacifiCare, through its chief operating officer, Jeff Folick, to underwrite the tournament in which Crane's company, Flo-Mac, Inc., was major sponsor. There were as many as two dozen annual corporate sponsors, with varying special awards or event holes, along with up to 26 raffle prizes, including two bats signed by tournament participant Tommy Davis, who won back-to-back National League batting championships with the Los Angeles Dodgers in 1962-63.

"My enjoyment came from all my participants having the best experience at a golf tournament, and Barbara spreading the word on needy children," Crane said. "It's very strange to look back at it and see how it progressed, along with the hours of preparation.

"As I passed the torch, my No. 1 rule was to reserve the date for next year. I sure miss Barbara and Joe," Crane said.

Among the many other names who aided the effort by playing in the event were former Los Angeles and Brooklyn Dodgers Maury Wills, Don Newcombe, Willie Davis and Jim "Junior" Gilliam, along with longtime USC football play-by-play man Tom Kelly, the aforementioned Mike Garrett and then-current major league pitcher Fernando Valenzuela. The format, as was customary in charity golf, was a best-ball scramble, with each participant getting three tee shots.

Occasionally, one of these notables would call the Obbema residence.

"One time, my son, Matt, picked up the phone and asked politely, like he was taught, who was calling," Obbema said. "When he said, 'Maury Wills,' Matt told him, 'no, who are you, *really*?' "

Matt Obbema, who now lives in Riverside County, Calif., developed into a promising professional wrestler but suffered the aforementioned testicular cancer. He was hospitalized to treat the cancer for 17 days, 11 of them in intensive care. While in the hospital, his condition was re-evaluated via a second opinion and, it turns out, he likely could have died if cancerous growths had not been removed.

Long before that, however, Matt had some proclivity for the mat at a very early age, it seems, and his sure-fisted dad inadvertently once became one of *his* punching targets.

"(He) gave me a black eye when he was 5 years old," Matt Obbema's father said. "I was showing him how to box, just kidding around, and I told him about always keeping up his guard.

"My wife at the time called me, and I dropped my hand, and Matt punched me right in the eye. The boy laughed at me like you wouldn't believe."

Tommy Davis recalls fondly his years after baseball of instead hitting golf balls for a good cause around either Tiger Woods's old haunt, the Navy course on the border between Cypress and Los Alamitos, Calif., or the Stallion Mountain layout in Las Vegas.

In fact, Davis, who wound up playing for a record (at the time) 10 major-league teams, offered Obbema a special nod each year at the tournament's awards banquet.

Davis always was the first to stand up and give Obbema an ovation when the latter took the microphone during the post-tournament awards dinner. "I felt he needed it because of the kind of guy he was," Davis said, in turn. "He knew a lot of entertainers and celebrities."

The key, Davis said, was helping foster children. "If we can get (it) across to kids – to the next generation – that's what we strive for," he said. Davis said he began such a role years before by playing in, or helping organize, charity events in his native New York City. (Davis graduated from Brooklyn's fabled Boys High, where he was a basketball teammate of future National Basketball Association Hall-of-Famer Lenny Wilkens, and classmate of members of the singing group Little Anthony and the Imperials.)

He said he and Obbema had met "years and years ago" in conjunction with the latter's successful trucking sales positions and Davis selling advertising specialties. (Interestingly, it was the same type client/business relationship that had enabled Obbema to hook up with Scott Crane.)

"He's an unforgettable person," Davis said of Obbema. Davis also joked that his friendship, and his longtime participation in the charity golf event, was really sealed in the event's later years "because my wife, Carol, liked him, too. She liked going to Las Vegas."

Similar to others close to Joe Obbema, Scott Crane has always marveled at how people misread him.

"A lot of my friends ask, "What do you see in him?', because they don't know. He has that big, bully, *macho*, SC-type of personality, but people who don't get to know him, misunderstand him completely," Crane said.

He said that Obbema is so pro-Trojan and anti-Bruin that "he told me to take a UCLA banner off the wall at my workplace." Yet if a Bruin or, say, a California Golden Bear, wanted to offer time to play in the tournament for the kids' sake, Obbema would be the first one waiting on the mat to welcome him.

In fact, one individual who always desired to play in the Obbema-organized golf tournaments, but was unable to, was Cal alumnus Jim Hanifan. He was in the midst of a long NFL coaching career, which included stints as head coach of the St. Louis (now Arizona) Cardinals, interim head coach of the Atlanta Falcons and numerous pro assistant coaching jobs.

"It seems like I always had some other commitment . . . and was tied up with other things," lamented Hanifan, who had been a star tight end for USC's rival Golden Bears in the mid-'50s, leading the nation in pass receptions with 44 in 1954.

The silver-haired, 79-year-old Hanifan, who lives in the St. Louis area and has been an analyst on St. Louis Rams' radio broadcasts, said he first met Obbema through their mutual friend, the late Craig Fertig. Fertig, a former USC quarterback, was a USC assistant coach when Obbema was a Trojan. Hanifan-Obbema was an instant and enduring friendship.

"He and I through the years became friends and have remained friends through the years," the ex-NFL head coach said of Obbema. "He is a genuine guy, a down-to-earth individual. You could tell by the way he handled the Fertig situation."

Hanifan was referring to ongoing efforts by Obbema and others to assist Fertig and his family in as many possible ways in conjunction with the latter's daughter's long battle with cerebral palsy.

Obbema said that the red-haired Fertig, who died of kidney failure at age 66 in October 2008, was an ebullient, self-effacing man, always willing to have fun at his own expense.

And *anyone* you talk to will only have laudable things to say about good-guy Fertig.

For instance, Obbema and former longtime USC assistant coach Dave Levy recall the one night in Orange County when they were helping ramrod a fundraiser to benefit payment of medical bills for Fertig's daughter.

As Levy tells the story, "There were about 600 people packed into the room, including John McKay, Mike Garrett and (fellow assistant) Marv Goux. All of us were scheduled to speak (including Fertig's friend Terry Donahue, the UCLA head coach and former playing rival).

"I was the first or second to speak, and I knew there were women in the room, so I made sure I warned them that I was about to use some rough language."

So here's what Levy told the attending throng: "When you talk about Craig Fertig, you always have to talk about John McKay. John McKay had a favorite word and that was 'cocksucker'. So for a long time, Craig told me that he thought that was his name."

On another occasion involving use of that favorite word, Obbema and Fertig were down in Miami to watch the Super Bowl, when they encountered McKay and longtime Kansas City Chiefs' Head Coach Hank Stram during a charity flag football game in which the two old veterans renewed their coaching rivalry. Obbema boasts that he was one of the few who had actually coached flag football and, therefore, was well-schooled in its nuances.

The squads were composed of former college and professional football players, with Obbema's team including the San Francisco 49ers' John Brodie as its quarterback. "The center was (Bob) Kuechenberg," whom Obbema had played against in the long Notre Dame-USC series. Kuechenberg was retired from the Miami Dolphins, who set an NFL record with a perfect season in 1972. Obbema said that while he knew the rules, Stram did not, including the fact that the center was eligible, and also there was no blitzing and no zone defenses.

"So I walked up to Coach McKay to tell him, and he said, 'Don't bother me.' Then I said, 'They're cheating' and he said, 'That cocksucker's cheating?'" At which point, McKay began listening to Obbema's advice to make any needed adjustments for the seven-man-per-side game, including throwing six straight center-eligible passes to Kuechenberg.

Fertig later was head coach at Oregon State from 1976-79, then spent years as a football broadcast analyst. On the night he passed away, USC remembered him with a moment of silence at the game against OSU's archrival Oregon Ducks.

One of Jim Hanifan's longtime coaching opponents with various NFL teams during a 45-year career was the late Jim Erkenbeck. The latter, who died of a brain aneurysm in March 2011 at age 81, lived not far from Obbema's Mater Dei High coach Dick Coury, north of San Diego, before moving further inland prior to his death.

"He epitomizes the perfect football player – strength, loyalty, toughness," Erkenbeck, then a college coach, said of Obbema before the retired coach's death. "I watched him at Mater Dei. I thought his SC time burned him out a bit. He's a very tough guy. He was very much a team guy. I really feel bad about him losing his physical prowess in recent years."

Erkenbeck, who had played in some of the S.A.F.E. golf tourneys, said Obbema evoked memories of one of his players when the veteran coach was employed by the Dallas Cowboys.

"Joe reminded me of a University of Washington player who played right tackle, Kevin Gogan," Erkenbeck said. "As a rookie, Gogan got into a bar altercation with someone who was badmouthing the Cowboys." Like Obbema, according to Erkenbeck, Gogan was merely defending his team's honor – nothing more, nothing less.

Gogan, who played 13 years in the NFL, wore his hard-nosed reputation on his sleeve, so much so that he received extra notoriety.

For instance, in an October 1998 feature on "The NFL's Dirty Dozen," a *Sports Illustrated* writer mused about Gogan, who was rated No.1 on that list:

> "Claim to shame: Goes off at wholly inappropriate moments. Will spice up practice by mauling teammates. 'He'll dive over the pile to hit you, even after the play,' says

Seahawks linebacker Darrin Smith. 'If you're anywhere near the pile, watch out.' "

Erkenbeck's comparison stopped short of saying his friend, Obbema, was ever called a dirty player by *anyone*; quite the contrary -- the old coach simply wanted to illustrate the Trojan's toughness by comparing him to another hard-as-nails Pac-8/Pac-10 player whom he had observed for years.

A veteran head football coach-turned-analyst – this one with a collegiate rather than pro background – never played in the golf tournament for another reason: Simply because he was not a golfer.

Seventy-three-year-old Harvey Hyde, now a radio commentator on ESPN's local Los Angeles affiliate, is a former head coach at Pasadena City College and the University of Nevada Las Vegas, who shifted into "retirement" by hosting Super Bowl parties in Las Vegas in the 1990s. That is when he and Obbema first met, then Obbema later appeared on Hyde's show approximately at least every other month, doing various commentary.

Hyde, who lives back in Pasadena with wife, Linda (same name as Obbema's spouse), said he is amazed at the former Trojan player's ability to network with almost anybody.

"My take on Joe: He's everybody's friend . . . like an information center," the coaching veteran said of Obbema's Forrest Gump-like proclivity to be seemingly everywhere and know so many people, in likening him to the popular fictional character in the Winston Groom novel, which was eventually was transformed into an Academy Award-winning motion picture. "He's Sports Central, not Sports Center, but Sports Central. He must be on the phone all day. He could take you through a guy's whole career. He knows everybody in the NFL."

Hyde likewise is keenly aware of Obbema's past avocation as a bouncer despite never having seen him in that action.

"If they had a major in college, he'd have his list; he'd be the dean of bouncers," he said. Hyde said he easily can envision his friend standing, St. Peter-like, at the door of a celestial bar holding a clipboard, all the while checking off names of prospective patrons.

In Hyde's mind, he and Obbema had met not *through* football, but *because* of football.

Despite not ever having coached at USC, Hyde admits that "I'm close to the Trojan Family." In addition to his daily sports radio show, he hosts a weekly USC pre-game show and the "Trojan Brunch" program during football season.

At Pasadena, Hyde coached several future Trojans, including defensive tackle Jon Loomis, later to be one of Joe Obbema's roommates and fellow bouncers.

During one of the Hyde-sponsored Las Vegas outings to the small casino town of Mesquite, 90 miles north of the Strip, is when one of the tragic moments Obbema faced throughout life occurred.

"While in Mesquite, we got word that Gary Magner had died," Obbema said. Magner was a defensive lineman who had been Obbema's teammate at both Mater Dei High and USC. One of Obbema's old Trojan teammates, ruddy-complected Rod Sherman, whose nickname was "Red Nose," had told him about the death. Sherman said Magner had a hip replacement. However, the ball socket was the wrong size and needed to be replaced.

"Gary visited the doctor and, while there, he was given a shot to thin his blood before the operation could be done," Obbema said. "The doctor left him for a few minutes and, when he returned, Gary had died of a blood clot that was caused by the shot."

One of Hyde's line coaches with the UNLV Rebels also became friends with Obbema after being introduced to him by their mutual friend, the aforementioned Chuck Dekeado, who had been a longtime consultant to Obbema's college coach, McKay – attesting further to the networking magic.

"He's a good guy," said Greg Mohns of Obbema. "Even though I didn't play or work with him, I know he was a hell of a football player," said Mohns, current assistant general manager and player personnel director with the Canadian Football League's Toronto Argonauts. Mohns (pronounced MAHNS), an American, spends half the year in Kansas City, where he grew up. When seeing Obbema over the years, it was "mostly social contacts," the kind on which Joe Obbema has continually thrived.

It always has been *that* simple – talk to someone, for *some* reason, and become their friend forever.

Obbema also cultivated other relationships resulting from all the time he spent on the golf course prior to becoming physically unable to regularly enjoy the sport and after he had ceased organizing the foster children's charity event.

Following his move to Las Vegas in the early 1990s, he joined the Jim Colbert-designed Stallion Mountain Golf Club and met a 30-year Navy retiree, Gene Alexander, whose career had been spent helping develop data processing programs for the Navy, Nevada Test Site and Atomic Energy Commission.

"Joe and I hooked up at the golf course," said the 83-year-old Alexander, who was a charter member of the club and still lives in Las Vegas. "We got thrown together in a foursome one day. The indoctrination to each other was who could tell the most jokes . . . and he said I was the only guy who could top him.''

So, according to instant-friend Gene Alexander, another unintended Obbema avocation had been birthed: Impromptu stand-up comic. (In an ironic twist, and proof that bloodlines hold true, Obbema's son, Matt, has embarked on a belated career in stand-up comedy.)

A big blow, among others, to Obbema and the entire Trojan Family was the 1995 death of wide receiver Bob Chandler, one of the best all-around athletes ever to wear a USC uniform and later a star with the Oakland Raiders and Buffalo Bills.

Adding to his pass-catching acumen, Chandler had been a top decathlete. Despite standing barely 6-foot-1 and never weighing more than 200 pounds, he high-jumped 6-foot-7, put the shot 57 feet and pole-vaulted 13 feet, according to his obituary in *The New York Times*.

In 1994, Chandler, although largely a non-smoker, began experiencing a nagging cough, and a rare strain of cancer was discovered in his lungs. He continued to work on Raider broadcasts while undergoing chemotherapy treatment at the USC Norris Center, but succumbed to the cancer on Jan. 28, 1995, at age 45.

Chandler had been one of the high school seniors, out of suburban Whittier, whom Obbema had helped try to recruit – successfully as it turned out – to USC, describing him as "one of the best. They had him stay in my dorm room" during the recruitment rush in 1969. "I wasn't sure I was gonna get my scholarship" because of a season-ending injury.

"We went to Julie's and had dinner, and I ended up getting my scholarship, and when they found out what kind of athlete he was, they tried to make him a quarterback. Then they realized what kind of hands he had, and he became a great receiver."

For most of his stay at USC, Chandler was the roommate and carbon-copy, size- and disposition-wise, of Obbema's Mater Dei and USC teammate, wide receiver Mike Morgan. Morgan, like Chandler, was a multi-talented athlete who excelled at virtually anything he tried and still possesses an even temper, level head and good sense of humor, according to those who know him best.

Obbema learned of Chandler's death at the Miami airport picking up his wife during a Super Bowl trip. The late Oakland owner Al Davis, a one-time USC assistant coach, was on the same plane and, while waiting for baggage, Davis got a call informing him of Chandler's death. Davis knew that Obbema and Chandler had been college teammates and told Obbema of the death.

"To Al's credit, he only stayed in Miami for one day and then returned to L.A. to help with the funeral arrangements," Obbema said of Davis, who died in October 2011 at age 82.

"I've known a lot of people," some of them the best in their sport, "and a lot of good athletes, but he (Chandler) was probably the best all-around athlete I've ever known," Obbema said.

At Chandler's funeral, "It was after O.J.'s first trial. A bunch of us were standing outside talking about our friend, Bobby, and I told Fertig we had to get going. Craig said he wanted to stay a little longer, and Al Cowlings said with a grin, 'I'll give you a ride.' Everybody started laughing." The laughter, of course, was in reference to the now-infamous, low-speed chase in the white Ford Bronco in which Cowlings had driven Simpson all over metropolitan Los Angeles with police pursuing them.

In the decade-plus of the golf tournament, one supposedly uneventful Saturday away from the links proved to be *very* eventful with a shocking blast from the past. It involved the above pursuit of the vehicle occupied by Joe Obbema's ex-teammates, Simpson and his "chauffeur," Cowlings.

Linda Obbema, Joe's second wife to whom he has been married about 25 years, remembers as if it were yesterday.

"It was a Saturday in 1992. We were working around our house in Buena Park," she said, "when the phone rang. It was a guy who was a friend named Jim Swofford.

"The phone kept ringing (with one call after another), and we began watching O.J. and Al on

TV. When I turned on the TV, (Joe) said, 'Oh, My God!' " Linda Obbema said that, just as she and her husband were starting to watch the big chase that stretched across Los Angeles and Orange counties, they noticed the vehicle on television was passing by right behind the wall that separated their backyard from the 91 (Riverside) Freeway.

As the phone would not stop ringing off the hook with call after inquiring call, Linda said she kept telling callers about Joe that "he's kind of tied up right now." Then Linda said, "I asked Joe, 'You gonna go and stop O.J.?', and he answered, 'Hell, no, he's got a gun'."

Joe Obbema said that, although Cowlings and Simpson were headed for some reason toward Costa Mesa, a city near Newport Beach, about 15 miles south, some erroneous reports indicated their destination instead was "Costa Rica." The circuitous pursuit, of course, wound up 40-plus miles to the west, back at Simpson's Brentwood estate in West Los Angeles, where Simpson's estranged wife, Nicole, and her companion, Ron Goldman, had been slain.

By the time Joe and Linda Obbema had moved to Las Vegas, Nev., later in the '90s, his back problems began to start bubbling back to the surface. Between 2004 and 2007, he underwent a total of four surgeries by a noted neurosurgeon named Jason Garber.

"The second surgery was caused because of an infection from a whirlpool," Obbema said. He said 3 ½-inch screws had to replace the 2 ½-inch variety. With even more sarcasm than his typically sarcastic self, Obbema said, "the fantastically wonderful UMC Hospital gave me a staph (staphylococcus) infection." Therefore, drains were inserted in his back, extending his hospital stay by four days, before Garber's physician's assistant ostensibly deemed him well enough to go home.

But alas, such a timely release was not advisable. You see, Linda Obbema did not get off work until 5:30 p.m., and, she was given not-good news by an attending physician, a USC graduate, like Joe Obbema, who had been perusing her husband's charts.

Linda Obbema had gone down to see how much longer it was going to take for the wheelchair to be delivered, and she noticed the doctor was reading her husband's files.

He explained to her that he was indeed an infectious-disease specialist – or the type of doctor who treats people with such maladies as HIV, staph and other serious infections.

He introduced himself and, believe it or not, his name was Dr. Skanky. Like any cardinal-blooded Trojan, he knew of his patient's football career. Skanky then explained to Obbema that the staph infection could possibly kill him.

When Skanky made it clear her husband would not be released that day, Linda replied, "I'm not going to tell him that; you tell him."

Then Skanky came to Obbema's room, reminding him that the very serious staph infection he had, if untreated, could likely prove fatal. He told Obbema that a nurse would come in within a half-hour and put antibiotics in his arm. After Skanky left, the nurse was a no-show, and repeated calls to other nurses and medical staff went unheeded.

"So I lay there all night because the orders were messed up," Obbema said. When the smoke had cleared, so to speak, his fellow former Trojan, rugby and coaching buddy Mike Eaton, who also was living in Las Vegas, came by to take him home.

The doctor had the antibiotics delivered to Obbema's home. The driver dropped off the machine, and a nurse came by the next day to set up

Obbema with a drip apparatus for home use but was not qualified to set up the apparatus.

"She told me I needed it ASAP or else I would die. I was scared out of my mind." For Joe Obbema, a guy who no one could scare – *ever* – it was a realization that perhaps for the only time in his life, he was truly terrified. "They hooked me back up and apologized.

"My friend, Ed Posthuma, took me to the doctor to have the staples removed after my first operation. I asked him how many staples they took out of my back, and he said all of them," Obbema said with a laugh. The tall (6-foot-7) Posthuma, a retired transmission operator for the Southern California Edison electric utility and Vietnam veteran, has been a major USC fan, driving his motor home from his Southern Nevada home to California to "tailgate" at Trojan home games for four decades.

"It was pretty much like Joe said. We went into this room" where doctors would remove the large, industrial-strength staples, Posthuma said. "Joe was so strong, and I helped hold him down. Joe was grimacing. It was horrible." Posthuma said he was so focused on helping restrain Obbema that he literally did not have time to count staples.

About a year after the near-death scare, a disc inside Obbema wore out, and Dr. Garber went back into insert a larger disc with new, 3 ½-inch screws. Then, following yet another year, with Obbema nearly completely healed, he went out to hit some golf balls just before attending a show at a casino not far from his home.

"Another guy and I slipped in the restroom. The other guy, Joe Duffy, was a paramedic, but I didn't find that out until later," he said. The casino issued a report.

After Obbema went back to Dr. Garber to update him, the doctor sent the patient to a radiologist's office, where a bruise was revealed, but it did not get better despite cortisone shots and other treatments. About four months later, a magnetic resonance imaging indicated that Obbema's injury was only a quarter of an inch from permanently paralyzing him, so surgeons inserted a bigger plate and six 4 ½-inch screws.

Obbema then was admitted to another hospital, he thought, but it seemed like he was at some posh resort instead – or maybe he had gone to Heaven and did not know it.

"It was a hospital called Mountain Vista. It's the best hospital I've ever been in," he said. "They delivered lunch in jacket-less tuxedoes. The nurse found a wheelchair that fit, I went home, and it took three years to heal." The last surgery, though, has exacerbated Obbema's arthritis, leading what he described as " 7 to 8 pain on a 1-to-10 range."

Many years before, in a different house just a few blocks away from Joe and Linda Obbema's home in the same Buena Park subdivision – the locals called them "tracts", and the *faux*-Spanish streets all were named "El" *this* or "El" *that* – is where Joe Obbema had grown up and nurtured his desire to be a big-time football player as one of the stars of the Buena Park Falcons. Obbema matured so fast that his siblings regarded him not just as a big brother but an important advisor/counselor and, at times, an occasional surrogate parent of sorts.

ONCE A TROJAN, ALWAYS A TROJAN

7

RAISING THE BROOD

I am the family face;

Flesh perishes, I live on.

-- Heredity, Thomas Hardy (1840-1928)

Amid all the varied roles Joe Obbema assumed – even while still a teen-ager – was that of a sometimes substitute "parent" to his two younger brothers and two younger sisters. Or at least he always proved to be an adviser with whom they could consult.

Brother Bob would have been almost 56 years old but died as a passenger in a motor-vehicle accident in California's Mojave Desert at age 33. Youngest sister Michele lost her battle with congestive heart failure at age 56 in January 2012. As was the case with Bob and Michele, the two surviving siblings of Joe Obbema are grateful in different ways to their sometimes-stern oldest brother for the care he showed in ensuring they all were loved even beyond maternal or paternal needs.

It was at times tempestuous, yet it was nonetheless unmitigated love – the kind that comes naturally.

"My father was a good man but not a father who taught me a lot," Joe Obbema said of his father, George, who died in 1998 at age 75. "He went to work every day and came home every day." The Obbemas' mother, Charline, was 78 when she passed away on a momentous date, Sept.12, 2001.

"My mom died the day after 9/11. She was awake and doing well, but I think after seeing what happened that day, she did not want to live anymore," Joe Obbema recalled. "We got a call that night about 10 p.m. telling us that she may not live very much longer, so we left and got to the hospital about 2:30 a.m., and she passed away about 7 that morning.

"It was two of the hardest days I have ever been through," Obbema admitted.

His sisters, Mary and Michele, agreed that their mother had been very patriotic and the widow of a decorated World War II veteran. So, already being ill and having watched what was perpetrated on the country she loved dearly on the day before she died, it could have hastened her death.

Many of the laudable traits of their parents seemed to rub off on Joe and his brothers and sisters. George Obbema was a loyal, hard worker in the Uniroyal Tires plant up the freeway toward Los Angeles in the City of Commerce. Charline Obbema had been a compassionate nurse, tending to others' woes, while raising five kids.

So the inherited characteristics were the industrial laborer's hard edge and persistence, coupled with the health-care provider's sympathetic touch.

At 10 years old himself, Joe started working and never stopped until later in life when partial disabilities prevented him from continuing full-bore. Even when he was playing football or being a hard-driving student, he worked at *something*, often in simultaneous multiple jobs. The first paycheck he earned was as a newspaper delivery boy.

Soon to follow was being the youngest box-boy ever at age 12 at nearby Farm Fair, then clean-up boy for a major supermarket chain. He did the clean-up job in the mornings before school after awakening daily no later than at 6 a.m., then went directly to Farm Fair from football practice to work from 3:30 to 7:30 p.m. That was followed by homework before going to bed nightly at 10. The lone concession to this lifelong regimen, Obbema said, was retiring at 11 p.m., rather than 10, most of the rest of his life.

While attending Mater Dei High School, a coeducational Catholic school owned then by the Archdiocese of Los Angeles (today by the Diocese of Orange), he paid his own tuition from the earnings at his various jobs. (In the 1970s, the campus was listed as the largest Catholic high school west of Chicago, with 2,220 students.)

"My first year at (the University of Southern California), they got me a job in a place storing steel products," he said. That was tailor-made for a strapping youth who weighed 225 pounds entering college and had expanded to 245 by his senior year.

Joe Obbema's four younger siblings attended mostly public schools, the one exception being sister Mary, who started at the nearby local parish school that her older brother had attended from third through eighth grades, St. Pius V. But young Mary soon was placed back in Buena Park public schools because a diagnosed heart murmur needed special attention. Joe's time at St. Pius had been preceded by attending St. John of God Catholic School across the Los Angeles County line in nearby Norwalk.

In her freshman year of high school, Mary attended Mater Dei, on a tuition-free waiver because her brother was an existing student/athlete, and was driven to and from school daily by Joe amid his otherwise-busy and productive schedule.

Regardless of which school they attended, each of Joe's siblings continually looked up to their older brother for daily guidance, advice or protection.

"Joe knows no strangers; he's (always) been that way; one of those guys," said Rick Obbema, at 54 the "baby" of the family despite having grown to 6-foot-4 and 250 pounds by the time he started playing college football in 1976. "He opens his door to everybody." For the past quarter-century, Rick Obbema has worked successfully in the technology industry in Northern California's Silicon Valley, currently as regional sales director for a computer-products firm.

Rick said one would have to look back at the tableau provided by their late father to understand the relationship the youngest Obbema, along with his two sisters and late brother, had with Big Joey, as they affectionately have always called him.

"My dad was a World War II veteran. He spent four straight years in the jungle" of the Pacific Theater, Rick said. "It's one of the reasons we're safe and free. He went in at about 16 or 17, then came back to raise a family." While fighting the Japanese hordes in the dense, muddy thicket of the Philippines, machine-gunner George Obbema earned the Bronze Star, more than one Purple Heart and other decorations.

George told his kids that there were times he and his fellow troops had to drink boiling water that dripped from the machine-gun barrel because they were underneath bunkers of Japanese soldiers, and could not sneak out, even for an occasional sip of cold water.

During that arduous existence, Papa Obbema, despite developing a hard-as-nails aura, wondered if he would ever come out of that morass intact. So he prayed – a lot.

"He vowed that if he got out of there alive, he'd name his first two children (if they were boy and girl) Joseph and Mary," George's elder daughter said.

Since it was mandated by the nuns who taught Catholic school pupils in those days to end anything they wrote with the initials "JMJ" – for Jesus, Mary and Joseph – someone asked Joe Obbema why his father did not name him Jesus instead.

With a straight face, Joe replied, "Because that name was already taken," demonstrating that lessons imparted on the class by the "sisters" who resembled penguins in their old-style habits had been absorbed well.

"Toil" should've been George Obbema's middle name because not long after exiting the torrid, horrid Pacific jungles, he did exactly *that*: Toiled for years in the giant Uniroyal plant southeast of downtown Los Angeles, literally pulling genuine rubber (not some artificial compound) to form tires. The rock-hewn plant, also known as The Citadel and just off the busy freeway, resembled an old-style castle, providing quite a conversation piece for his family. The plant closed in 1978 and by 1990 was converted into a retail site known as The Citadel Outlets.

"Uniroyal looked like a castle when we went down to visit. I wondered: Why was my dad working in a castle?" Mary said. "I know his hands were really callused."

"One time, we bought him a carving knife to cut the Thanksgiving turkey, and it couldn't cut his hands because they had so much rubber on them," Rick said.

After each of those family dinners, sister Michele/Shelly said the kids learned how to play poker with their parents and grandparents.

George and Charline eventually moved their family from suburban Norwalk a little farther down Interstate 5 (the Santa Ana Freeway to old-timers) to the newer Orange County "burb" of Buena Park, where their kids grew up. That first house the family bought there on El Cerro Drive cost $13,700 in the late '50s.

Rick said he watched his oldest brother carefully despite their 10-year age difference, never worrying about whether Joe was looking back through the corner of his eye.

"He was a sounding board for me to go up and talk to. I would discuss choices with Joe," Rick said. "Joe used to get up early in the morning, around 4 or 5 a.m., to move trash" in his supermarket job.

By the time the family's little "baby" had hit age 13, he already had matched his muscular, 23-year-old brother in height.

"I was lucky because I was the biggest and the strongest," Rick said. Even so, he always deferred to Joe when it came to seeking advice.

As Rick was scheduled to enter his junior year at Buena Park High School -- from which his sister, Michele, and brother, Bobby, graduated -- he consulted with his parents. George and Charline allowed their youngest to move in with their oldest. Joe was finishing pursuit of his teaching certificate and was a part-time coach at West High, 30 miles away in Torrance, while also holding down a bouncer job at a club, the Front Page.

Charline, although not an athlete herself, bred a brood that included not only three football-playing sons but perhaps the best on-field and on-court performer in the family, Michele.

"My sister Michele was an incredible athlete, a great softball player," Rick said. "She'd be one of the best girl athletes (if she were competing now)." He said if Title IX, the federal education-equalization law that became effective in 1972, had been on the books when Michele played, it would have been quite different.

Moreover, despite not being a participant, Mama Obbema "knew sports better than any one of the moms around there," Rick said. She and George would take the younger kids to as many of Joe's games as possible, given the arduous schedule of two working parents with five children.

"I saw every one of Joe's USC (home) games," said Rick, adding that it was a special treat, outside of simply watching the brother whom he almost worshipped.

"The best way to put it, the guys at SC during that period (mid- to late-'60s), they could've beaten most opponents, they were so good." He did not mean just the starters but the highly adept athletes like his brother who stocked every backup position on the Trojans' loaded-for-Bear (or Bruins) roster.

As one of Joe Obbema's USC teammates, Dick Allmon, had once put it, "The difference between playing and not playing was an eyelash."

When Rick had completed a stellar season at West High, with his size and speed, he was the top "blue chip" prep running back in the country. Therefore, he pretty much had his choice of colleges. He chose UCLA, however, attributable mostly to the efforts of Head Coach Dick Vermeil and Bruins' recruiting coordinator Carl Peterson. Vermeil eventually led the St. Louis Rams to the Super Bowl title and previously had lured Rick Obbema to a free-agent signing with the Philadelphia Eagles before Obbema was released on the team's final cut; Peterson was the Kansas City Chiefs' longtime general manager until 2009.

At UCLA, Rick, who had been converted to linebacker, suffered some injuries and felt he was not treated well by Head Coach Terry Donahue. So he followed Bruin defensive coordinator Dick Tomey, who until 2009 was head coach at San Jose State, to the University of Hawaii. Rick Obbema was a consistent letterman for the Rainbow Warriors and earned a Bachelor's Degree in finance and marketing.

"Joey's a really good guy," said youngest sister, Michele, a few months before her January 2012 death. When their mother died, Michele, whom everyone knew as "Shelly," took over the Buena Park house in which they all had grown up – the one George and Charline bought for less than $14,000, little more than a half-century before. A single woman all her life, Shelly rented out the extra space to roomers. One of her biggest daily hurdles since the 2008 presidential election was fending off mindless people who heard "Michele Obbema" and immediately thought "Michelle Obama."

"I get the Michelle Obama crap all the time. Don't go there," she lamented.

Shelly, six years younger than Joe, said the entire clan takes great pride in its "Heinz 57" roots –

Dutch on their father's side, and a mixture of Irish, English and a touch of Native American from their mother's ancestors, most notably the O'Malleys.

Shelly's sister, Mary, said that within the paternal side of their family, there have been two schools of pronunciation of their last name. *These* Obbemas – George's bunch – have always pronounced it OH-BEE-MUH. *Those* Obbemas – George's relatives back in his native state of Illnois – prefer UBB-BIM-UH. Anyway you cut it, it's Dutch to me.

As is well-documented, Shelly said Joe is the one who held the family together when "Bobby" had his fatal crash; being listed as next-of-kin, it was Joe's sacred duty to apprise the rest of the Obbemas of their dear brother's death.

Shelly was hit hardest when Bob died because "we did everything together; he even dated some of my friends," she said. Relatives insist the two were also the most athletically gifted in this sports-minded family.

Speaking about Joe, she said, "He was a great big brother. He's my hero. He supported me by attending my college games," despite his own studies, Division I football responsibilities and ongoing multiple job obligations. "He gave me great support; he's always been there for me."

In turn, Shelly would go watch all her biggest brother's games, even trying unsuccessfully to get into the locker rooms, which did not allow entry to females, related or not.

"People used to tell me that I played like a boy. I was always picked before the boys in pickup games," said Shelly, who earned a graphics and design degree from Cal State Fullerton, to which she transferred after earning volleyball player of the year honors at Cypress (Junior) College.

Shelly Obbema's athletic résumé included being a 16-points-per-game point guard in basketball, a hitter in volleyball despite standing a setter's height of only 5-foot-6, and a versatile softball player. One of her slightly younger contemporaries was Ann Meyers. The widow of Los Angeles Dodgers' pitcher and broadcaster Don Drysdale starred at Sonora High School in nearby La Habra, then was the first to break into the women's college basketball ranks via Title IX with the first full athletic scholarship awarded to a woman at UCLA in the early 1970s. Most recently, she has been known as Ann Meyers Drysdale, and became general manager of the Women's National

Basketball Association's Phoenix Mercury in 2006.
They won the 2009 WNBA title.

Like the Obbemas, Meyers Drysdale was
from a large Catholic family – with 11 children.
After her sophomore year at Cornelia Connelly, an
all-girls' Catholic school in Anaheim, Meyers
transferred to public Sonora High in La Habra,
where older brother David also starred three years
previously before likewise going on to UCLA and
later playing for the NBA's Milwaukee Bucks. In
light of her older brother's ability, it was interesting
that Meyers Drysdale was the only woman to sign a
free-agent contract with an NBA team, the Indiana
Pacers, in 1979.

While earning All-America basketball honors
in her four seasons as a Bruin, Meyers Drysdale also
competed in her freshman year as a high-
jumper/pentathlete on a national champion track and
field squad, then punctuated her college sports
career her junior and senior years as a volleyball
middle-hitter.

"Actually, track was my first love, but I was
on a basketball scholarship," she said, sounding a
lot like all-around high-school rival Shelly Obbema.

The Meyerses' oldest sister, Patty, "was
instrumental in opening the door" for Title IX and

the expansion of women's sports by virtue of her play as the starting center on the 1970 Cal State Fullerton team that won a women's national collegiate championship, Meyers Drysdale said. "She went on to play professional softball in Florida and became a teacher for over 30 years."

"We played a lot against each other in each sport, and we always guarded each other," Shelly said of Meyers Drysdale. One of Shelly Obbema's classmates when she was a multi-sports star at Buena Park High was a fellow named Steven Seagal, whose later pursuits are well-known -- the most recent was a cable TV series that chronicled his heretofore-fairly-unknown exploits as a longtime reserve deputy sheriff in post-Katrina suburban New Orleans, followed by possibly running for office in his newer home state of Arizona.

"She hit a home run one time off that famous softball pitcher who was the Queen in the King and his Court – that's how good she was," Joe said of Shelly. If you might doubt that Shelly Obbema was an athletic peer to her physically bigger brothers, go ask John G. Smith, brother Joe's 6-foot, 200-pound-plus, off-campus roommate at USC.

"We were drinking once at Joe's parents' house in Buena Park" when it still was relatively acceptable to drink and drive, Smith said. "I was pretty much shit-faced drunk and announced that I was leaving. As I started to cross the front yard, Michele tackled me and kept me down on the ground" so that Smith couldn't leave – and drive drunk.

Shelly said George Obbema, who had been a Little League coach and semi-pro baseball player as a teen-ager just before World War II, "helped a lot" by showing each of his children the nuances of sports when they were young.

Mary Trask was bitten by the Big Love Bug early. She met a sailor named David Trask when she was 16, and has been married to him ever since – for 46 years. Not long afterward, she earned her high-school equivalency as a Navy wife, as they moved to places such as Bremerton, Wash., and Albuquerque prior to returning permanently to Orange County.

But even before that, the 62-year-old No. 2 kid in the Obbema clan had formed her values, simply by being around her close-knit family. Again, if anybody dared mess with his younger siblings, they would have had to face Joe Obbema.

Case in point: "I remember one time before I got married, I was dating a guy who's in the band,

and the guy brought me home late," Mary said. "Joe and some other football players were out front because my dad was mad (and waiting inside the house). They picked up his Volkswagen and put it back down, telling him to never let it happen again."

"What I actually told him was if he had balls enough, he could come back and date my sister again," Joe said. And apparently the young suitor possessed that testicular fortitude.

"I never thought I'd see the guy again, but he came the next night for another date," Mary said.

A few years later, in 1975, Mary and David were living in nearby Garden Grove in the first house they had bought.

David Trask noticed some kids across the street with a bag. A cop came out to check and the cop got blinded temporarily by a "bomb," so the Trasks naturally tried to help him. For their trouble, they were victimized by a "Molotov cocktail" thrust through one of their windows because they were potential witnesses. The Trasks soon sold the house and "the gangsters burned down the house the day after we sold it," Mary said, the young thugs not knowing the family had moved.

Think that was enough for one family? Think again.

In what Mary Trask regards as sheer coincidence 15 years later when living in West Covina, a San Gabriel Valley community over the hill to the north from Orange County, around Christmastime, a baby-sitter's son was playing with a lighter and some coiled *menorah* candles used for the Jewish holiday of *Hanukah*. Instead of the candles flickering in the eight-hole candelabra as intended for the "Festival of Lights," they burned down the Trasks' *entire* house.

"Luckily, we had good homeowners' insurance," said Mary Trask, who now lives near Joe's oldest son, Matt, in Norco, east of Orange County, where she can raise and run her horses.

About a year later, in between the West Covina blaze and Norco, however, Mary and David and their two kids were victims once more of an unplanned minor disaster.

"Whoever built the house put in temporary coupling, and the roof caved in. We had to live in a motel," she said.

"We finally decided we'd always have acreage in Riverside County (Norco)" for the horses, Mary said. The early heart murmur and subsequent childhood heart surgery, which prevented Mary Obbema Trask from being as athletic as she desired, resulted in her becoming such a passionate horsewoman.

She said the secret to brother Joe being the way he is boils down to something simple: "He always liked to have people around him."

When Joe and Linda were married in 1989, Joe had his two children and the two children of his late fiancée, Mo, and Linda had three children – a scenario right out of *Yours, Mine and Ours*. They started conducting family meetings soon after Linda moved in, with three families merging into one. Joe and Linda concur that the meetings were most helpful with the number of children coming and going.

Joe Obbema remembers clearly one of their first meetings before the wedding. "We were having the meeting so that everyone would know what was expected of them at the wedding," he said. He warned them that if anyone "screws up, you're gonna think that Genghis Khan is a damn altar boy."

Brave little Wendy, the youngest in the entire blended brood and also the youngest of Linda's three biological offspring, had no clue as to whom Genghis Khan was, so when the *paterfamilias* had concluded his speech, Wendy shot her hand straight in the air and, vowing to "be good," then asked, "Who is Genghis Khan?"

Linda Obbema tells of a time when her husband was out of town on business and she returned home for work to find all the bowls and glasses sitting dirty in the kitchen sink. Even though no one admitted to having eaten at home that day, Linda told the kids how funny it was that all the bowls and glasses jumped into the sink by themselves.

"I then went out, bought plastic bowls and glasses, and printed each child's name on them so that here would be no mistake about whom they belonged to," she said of the impromptu, color-coordinated "dinnerware."

There was another family meeting after Joe Obbema returned from out of town.

"I had prepared this entire list of things for them to do. There were nine kids, counting my sister Mary's two, so we had a lot to talk about," he said.

Eric Bessette, among the oldest and the only son of Joe Obbema's late fiancée Mo, had just started working at nearby Disneyland and arrived a little late. At the Magic Kingdom, one of the jobs he had was working in the costuming department, helping dress Disney characters. So when he walked in with the meeting already started, he may have felt he still was at Disneyland in the Mad Hatter's realm, with the bowls and glasses in place in front of each child's place at that table for what turned out to be a weekly gathering. The family meetings were "good roundtable discussions," Eric said.

"Right before I went into my tirade," Joe said, "Wendy leaned over and asked Eric what the bowls are for. He whispered that 'he is so pissed off that he's going to knock all your teeth out and put them in the bowl.' Wendy then looked at her new big brother and asked what the cups are for. He looks at her with a straight face and said, 'to rinse.'"

Obbema said he could not help but crack up. "It just blew my entire tirade," he said. Then, with a calmer demeanor than had been planned, he reminded each of their specific responsibilities – thanks, of course, to Wendy's unintended mood-changer.

For Wendy's part, it was simpler than that, being only 8 years old at the time. "I was worried more about the toy in the cereal box," she admitted.

It was important to be able to laugh – at the others or yourself, said Eric, now 41, married and residing just down the road from Matt Obbema and Mary Trask in neighboring Lake Elsinore. "Everybody had to get a quick wit because if you could laugh at Joe," it would defuse any potentially explosive situation.

Today, Wendy Nicklos, 33, also married and living in Conway, Ark., north of Little Rock, admits that, despite her stepfather being sometimes stubborn about discipline, "I don't think I'd be the person I am today" without his guiding hand.

When Joe proposed to Linda, she had been living with her three children in a rough neighborhood and was working multiple jobs. "He always sacrifices for us," said Wendy, who, like her mother did, plans to open her own day-care facility.

"He was always working his ass off . . . taking care of his family," blood or otherwise, Eric said. "There was a whirlwind of everything" when Mo died, including Mo's daughter and Eric's older sister, Beverly, just having gotten married. Eric was taken in by Joe and Linda Obbema, without qualification, as one of their own, "for the right reason," Eric said.

What sister Mary said about being surrounded with people has worked well with other kids for Joe Obbema – even if they were not his own, or his brothers or sisters, and even if it required much extra effort.

After a few years of marriage, Linda changed from working out of the house to working in the home, and she started a day-care center. The older girls already were married, and the young charges included some members of the resident blended family, among them grandchildren, who always called Joe "Papa."

One day, Joe Obbema recalls, he offered to help with the day care so that Linda could take a now-much-older Wendy to a deposition that was supposed to last only a couple of hours but wound up going about five hours.

So here is this big man – well over 6 feet tall and already having easily passed 225 pounds several years previously – with a roomful of six children, the youngest a pair of six-month-old twin boys, the oldest no more than three or four years old.

"One of the things the kids loved were stories," he said. Then, as the day lengthened, one kid asked Big Joe, aka "Papa," to tell him a story. "So I had to watch the kids for her," he said. "I started the story with *The Three Pigs* and then added *Little Red Riding Hood,* and finally, to keep it going and spice it up and make it more interesting, I threw in *Superheroes*." This lasted more than an hour.

"When I finished, they were all gathered around and one of them yelled, 'Papa, tell us another one.' When Linda finally got back and she walked in, I told her it was torture; I was exhausted but content."

"He went to a local restaurant that had a bar," Linda said.

Now that the other members of the extended Obbema family are all well into adulthood, they bear varied but loving recollections of "back in the day."

For instance, Mo's 44-year-old daughter, Beverly, now married with the last name of Pulos, lives in the Washington. D.C., area, where she works for a title insurance company.

"He's been an awesome grandfather to my sons (Damian, 20, and Camden, 19)," Beverly said of Joe. "They used to climb in bed to eat popcorn and watch football with him. He's been a great guy. It's always been a great experience being his daughter.

"Both Joe and Linda have great big hearts."

Linda's other two birth-children are Holly Sinders, 45, and Nathan Kennett, 35, both of whom reside in Central Texas, not far from where they lived for parts of their childhood and also fairly close to Joe and Linda.

Holly already was a young adult who was engaged and living in the Boston area when her mother called to tell her she was engaged to Joe. Today, she finds it helpful for her 18-year-old son, Dayne, to have Grandpa close by to share his own football stories and give advice to the budding long-snapper and interior lineman. In fall 2013, Dayne was ticketed to attend Missouri's Southern Baptist University on a football scholarship.

"There's always a challenge" with a large, blended family, Holly said. "I was in a unique position" as she was already out of the house. "He opened his home without a catch. Joe's got a good heart. Those years of his S.A.F.E. service" with the annual golf tournament benefitting foster children "were very honorable."

Despite inherent initial skepticism and cynicism on the young man's part, Nathan said Joe helped him get a grocery warehouse job, but for sports-minded Nathan there was another occasion that left a lasting, and positive, impression.

Holding back tears, Nathan said, "My freshman year (of high school),(Joe) got me tickets to a (Los Angeles) Lakers game, introduced me to Magic Johnson, and got a lot of Laker autographs and happy-birthday posters."

The only regret Nathan has in his long and mostly pleasant relationship with his stepfather occurred years ago when they got into a dinnertime altercation that momentarily turned physical after Nathan moved back to California.

Quite contrary to that single instance, Nathan said, "When I was there, I was treated as family."

Even though he stands only 5-foot-9, Nathan enjoyed being a small-forward when he played basketball, and has now shifted gears from being a correctional officer in Nevada to a newly graduated massage therapist in his native Texas.

Joe Obbema's younger child of his two biological kids is Mary Jo, the same age as stepbrother Nathan.

Living and working in San Bernardino County, Calif., she helps workers' compensation patients in medical-related court cases.

Like her non-blood siblings, she echoes fondness and admiration for her father. "He's a great dad with lots of fond memories. He worked hard and was always there for us," Mary Jo, also known as "Me-Jo," said. He provided "good discipline and care. He's a good role model for being a parent, even though everybody has problems. He recognizes he was always doing his best despite difficulties."

While every individual or family bears certain burdens, Mary Jo said her father experienced more than his share: The anorexia struggles of her birth-mother; the death of Mo; his younger brother's and sister's premature passing; his mother's death; and his own near-death scare, culminated in later years by his battles with varied ongoing pain.

As for her stepmother, Mary Jo described Linda Obbema as "amazing." Because of both Linda and Joe, the idea that kids from different families could be one was engendered on a daily basis. "It manifested itself best at holidays," Mary Jo said.

She said it was "a weight off the shoulders" when her biological parents split due to the "obsession" and physical and emotional toll the eating-disorder problems constantly presented. (Joe Obbema's ex-wife lives in Illinois.)

Attributable largely to the after-effects of his testicular cancer, former professional wrestler Matt Obbema, who turned 37 in 2013, sometimes feels he is in a pain contest with his father.

One previous missed diagnosis revealed the need for only chemotherapy, when 10 ½-hour lymph-node surgery actually was required.

"I almost died twice during the operation. Both lungs collapsed and my heart fluttered" during the 27 days in the hospital, Matt said. For a year after the surgery, Matt battled an addiction to pain-killers; he lost his house, then had to end his wrestling career, and lost a subsequent job as a nightclub disc jockey.

For now, Matt is close to an Associate's Degree in criminal justice and is a budding stand-up comic and committed vegan. He is proud his father was sometimes tough on him and his various brothers and sisters.

"He disciplined us normally . . . He was a real man; he wasn't a sissy," Matt said. So many current parents don't raise their kids to become adults. Parents today are more interested in making things easy for themselves by being buddy-buddy."

The Obbema children always were in bed early, unlike today's increasingly coddled youngsters who often are out late on weeknights with their parents or not.

When Matt talks about if Joe Obbema were not "the type of man he was, I would've been dead," he and his father always joke about it, with Joe taking it as a supreme compliment. For some time, father-son tension existed when Joe regarded pro wrestling as "fake," never wanting to get fully involved with the activity.

Matt, however, ultimately understood, saying, "When you get older, you start to appreciate some things your father did."

8

WHEN A MONARCH IS KING

I am the monarch of all I survey,

My right there is none to dispute.

--Verses Supposed to Be Written by Alexander Selkirk (1782), st. 1, William Cowper (1731-1800)

Despite doctor's orders forbidding him from playing football his freshman year at Santa Ana's Mater Dei High, faith and forbearance made Joe Obbema determined to do otherwise.

Standing almost 6-foot-2 and already weighing over 200 pounds as he entered his sophomore year, Obbema knew with dead certainty that the painful reverse sit-ups he did daily for nearly the past year would be his "secret" to returning to the football field.

Veteran head coach Dick Coury realized that, of all the truly great high school players he had mentored, Obbema was likely the most persevering, if not the most talented in his own way.

So Coury truly looked forward to having the gritty, two-way player available on the varsity for the 1964 season. The '63 season found Obbema on the sophomore squad before being promoted to the varsity his final two years.

Before he was diagnosed with a serious knee ailment known as osteochondritis, Obbema had showed signs of being what Coury termed "something truly special." In drills up to the point of the dire diagnosis that had sidelined him, he was able to dominate offenses from basically an outside linebacker position, and demonstrated potential to be a steady short-yardage puncher as a fullback.

Obbema dabbled at playing some tight end as a junior and scored only one touchdown. The one score was notable, though; it occurred on a deep-post pattern when quarterback Pete Sanchez found him wide-open.

By the time he was a senior, Obbema became the starting fullback and earned All-Orange County

and All-California Interscholastic Federation
Southern Section honors, scoring 19 touchdowns his
senior year in 1965 to help lead the Monarchs to the
CIF 5A title.

(Mater Dei is one of only two high schools in
history – and the only non-public school – to
produce two Heisman Trophy winners: Notre
Dame's John Huarte in 1964 and USC's Matt
Leinart in 2004. Woodrow Wilson in Dallas, Tex.,
is the only other high school to have two future
Heisman winners in quarterback Davey O'Brien at
Texas Christian in 1938 and wide receiver Tim
Brown at Notre Dame in 1987.)

However, in the time heading into that
championship season after Obbema had been given
a second life in the sport in which he excelled, he
was the tacit and acknowledged leader on a team
chock-full of leaders. Coury and the Mater Dei
assistant coaches never had to prompt Joe Obbema;
he merely took the lead consistently without ever
being told to do so. After all, there were valid
reasons why he was designated team captain.

"The biggest thing about Joe Obbema is his
work ethic. He never gave up. It's the difference
between being an average player and a better
player," said Sanchez, the 1965 CIF Co-Player of
the Year, who moved on to the USC football team

with Obbema. If the Monarchs were a giant wheel with a lot of talented spokes, Sanchez certainly was the hub of the wheel, with his versatility in being dangerous in either passing or running situations. And if it were possible to have a second hub, it would have been Obbema. "I remember one day Coach (John) McKay told Joe, 'Obbema, if you had the same talent as what's in your heart, then no one could block you.'

"As a quarterback, I was always in charge on the field. After the third or fourth game (of his sophomore year), coach (Coury) let me audibilize (change plays at the line of scrimmage, if needed)," Sanchez said.

At USC, Sanchez was destined to be the first Sanchez (long before recent quarterback Mark Sanchez, no relation) to call signals as a Trojan starter. However, his right knee locked up as a freshman, then he redshirted his sophomore season before an even worse fate befell him. On a summer trip with two friends to Ensenada, Mexico, in August 1968, the Volkswagen van he was driving rolled over, with Sanchez's other knee pinned under the clutch. Another American tourist was able to use an axe to pry the knee loose from the rubble, and Sanchez was taken to a Mexican hospital, where a dirty ACE bandage was applied and stayed on his leg for two days.

When he arrived at a San Diego hospital, a pin was inserted through his ankle with his foot put in traction. That was followed by two weeks at a hospital in Anaheim, near Sanchez's Santa Ana home, plus six more months in a wheelchair and two years on crutches. In other words, a promising football career had ended. However, Sanchez eventually met his future wife, Kathy, went to work for the Postal Service for 34 years, and has been married for more than 40 years with three sons a product of that long and fruitful union.

Coury, whom Sanchez termed "a great person," called to check on him every day, as did USC Coach McKay. In addition, such teammates as O.J. Simpson, Bob "Reb" Brown and a fellow named Joe Obbema offered consolation and support.

"Joe was always supportive. He was at the hospital every day after my first knee injury, and he said he wanted to kick my ass for letting the Ensenada thing happen," Sanchez said.

Like his pupil Obbema, Coury's magnanimity was not selective; when compassion was warranted, the old coach never had to be asked – he acted. For example, after the 95-year-old father of another

Monarch-turned-Trojan, big defensive lineman Steve Pultorak, died not long ago, Coury quietly showed up at the funeral to offer condolences. "We hugged and had a good talk," said the 63-year-old Pultorak, who still is a teacher at Royal High, not far from the Reagan Presidential Library in Simi Valley, Calif. "Every good coach is a good teacher, just like Dick," said the 6-foot-3 Pultorak, who used to pay gas money with other Monarch football players when they rode to school daily from Buena Park and Anaheim in Obbema's 1957 Chevrolet, a car that always was filled to capacity with teammates.

As 10th-graders, prior to the "chauffeur-driven" Chevy, Obbema and his classmates who played football hitchhiked home each day after practice along busy 17th Street, eventually finding certain drivers who recognized them and offered rides. That was following a freshman year when Obbema was only 14 and was relegated to riding the bus on the 20-mile round-trip to and from his Buena Park home.

Even before the '65 championship, in 1962, there was quarterback Huarte, a traditional right-handed thrower. Then much later, in 2004, Mater Dei quarterback product Leinart, this time a left-hander, won the Heisman as a USC Trojan. Huarte's prep coach, Coury, also coached at Mater Dei in the mid-1960s a future USC wide receiver named Bruce Rollinson, who for the past 24 years has been the supremely successful Monarch head football coach in the Coury tradition.

Rollinson's most recent team was 11-3 in 2012, losing in the Pac-5 finals to Long Beach Poly, and he was named Orange County Coach of the Year, according to materdei.org, the school's official website. Since Rollinson became head coach in 1989, the Monarchs have won more than 200 games, including five CIF-SS championships, 15 league titles and two mythical national championships.

All told, the Monarchs are 480-187-6, with 26 league titles, nine CIF-SS titles, two *USA Today* national championships, five undefeated seasons and only five losing seasons in nearly six decades of football.

When Obbema's Monarch team won the '65 title, it was a precursor and almost carbon copy of the '67 championship season for Obbema at USC. Mater Dei marched through its schedule with a single blemish, a regular-season, 20-20 tie on the road against league rival St. Paul. Similarly, USC in '67 had its ring-bearing run marred by one stumble, the 3-0 conference loss in the mud at Oregon State.

The squad shut out three opponents in 1965, including Centennial, 21-0, in the CIF championship game, and six other opponents were held to one touchdown en route to a 12-0-1 record.

The Mater Dei roster was deep in talent. In addition to Obbema, Sanchez and Pultorak and the late fellow future Trojan defensive lineman Gary Magner, the team included the likes of such gifted offensive players as Rollinson, whose track record is self-evident; Mike Morgan, yet another Monarch-turned-Trojan; tackle Ronnie Brown; and center Bill Smith, a Mater Dei product who moved on to USC but had his playing career cut short similar to Sanchez's fate after a motorcycle accident between his freshman and sophomore years. Brown, the oldest of Bart and Sue Brown's 16 children who resided near the Obbemas, was Coury's nephew; he, too, was ticketed for possible stardom at USC when he fractured his neck in a near-fatal dive off a Newport Beach pier into three feet of water.

Along with being a key blocker and scoring all those touchdowns, Obbema was the star linebacker, who also blocked 14 punts and six extra-point or field-goal attempts in 1965.

The sophomore who spelled him was Eric Patton, now 63 and longtime successful head coach at San Clemente High after a playing career at Notre Dame.

"I played the same position as Joe. He needed rest on defense because of so much time he spent on offense," said Patton, who also teaches English.

Henry Enriquez, the CIF Player of the Year as an Obbema-like fullback on one of Coury's first championship teams in the late '50s, when Mater Dei won back-to-back CIF championships, also later was a part-time Monarch assistant coach when Obbema played.

Enriquez said Obbema possessed Jekyll-and-Hyde-like qualities. "He was a nice, polite young man off the field – a good guy who changed when he put on a football uniform."

Young Obbema already was so intense as a sophomore that it sometimes manifested itself in vigilante-like proportions. There was the case, for example, when sophomore-team coach Enriquez read a letter from upcoming opponent Long Beach Poly that stated the Jackrabbits would "kick the fish eater's ass." That referred to the then-centuries-old practice of Catholics to refrain from eating meat on Fridays. Enriquez told his charges that "we don't want anyone making fun of our team or religion."

Then, on the game's first play, Obbema hit the Poly ball-carrier hard, upending him, and yelling at the opponent something about beating "fish-eaters." That prompted Enriquez to quickly grab Obbema and admonish him: "Joey, Joey, *I* wrote the letter. Don't kill nobody!" (Similar to Clint Eastwood's admonition to Obbema years later.)

The 74-year-old Enriquez, a retired school teacher who played collegiately at Utah and later at San Diego State under the late Don Coryell, further described Obbema as "a natural, strong, emotional football player. If you ever got in his way, you'd wind up second best. He was like an animal" on the field, Enriquez said.

Morgan, who was a junior during the '65 season, carried it a step further about Obbema with an animal analogy. "He was tough; you couldn't bring him down. He was like a bull. He didn't run right but ran straight up," said Morgan, whose fraternal twin, Jim, was on the same Monarch squad before moving on to play at Santa Ana College and Tulsa.

The 6-foot-1, 175-pound Morgan, now 64 years old, also said that he and Rollinson, Mater Dei's speedier deep threats in a modified veer offense, used to joke a lot in the huddle, but that Obbema always was deadly serious and harbored an extra shot of determination, it seemed. Because he was much bigger than Morgan or Rollinson, Obbema consistently was given the ball deep into the "red zone" and just as consistently scored so many short-yardage touchdowns.

"On double-days (two-a-day drills), we had 'Murderer's Row,' and running backs had to tackle other running backs, so I dreaded having to tackle Joey, and having him tackle me," Morgan said.

Coury said of Morgan, "He was a great all-around athlete. Had he not been injured at SC his senior year," he would have likely played in the National Football League. However, his damaged knee would not hold up when Coury, then a Denver Broncos' assistant, convinced the team to try him out in pre-training camp.

Eric Patton remembers the tie at St. Paul as "a very, very emotional game" punctuated by controversy in the final seconds. He said what happened was a seminal moment that inspired him to eventually take up teaching and coaching as a profession.

As Mater Dei lined up to try and kick what would have been a short field goal to win the game, the officials, for whatever reason, would not permit it. So Coury, who rarely lost his cool, went nose-to-nose with the referee, insisting the decision was wrong. Patton was impressed by his head coach so vehemently defending his team, saying "it was an inspirational moment in that season." (Patton, incidentally, is one of only eight Monarchs selected as *Parade* magazine High School All-Americans, the third most of any school since the publication began choosing such "dream" teams in 1965. According to parade.com, the magazine's website, Mater Dei is the nation's sixth-ranked all-time prep football program.)

"They let the clock run out before our kicker, Greg Huarte (John's younger brother), could attempt a short field goal. He was good enough that he would have made it easily," Coury lamented.

Greg's older brother, John, concurred with his old coach, regarding his younger sibling's pinpoint toe. "Greg was a very good kicker," the Heisman winner said. "He was very accurate up to 35 to 40 yards or more. All the short stuff was easy," John Huarte said of his brother, who went on to kick for the St. Mary's College Gaels in Moraga, Calif., and in 2010 survived critical brain surgery to combat an aneurysm.

The field-goal incident so enraged the determined Monarchs that they did not lose another game en route to an eventual CIF title by beating shifty, UCLA-bound running back Mickey Cureton and Centennial of Compton in the championship game at the Los Angeles Coliseum.

In advancing, Mater Dei had benefited from a confusing call in a 17-14 quarterfinals win over fellow Orange County school Westminster when an apparent opposing touchdown scored by future Trojan George Berg was called back. An official blew his whistle, causing Monarch defenders to pause, "and that's why that guy scored," Morgan explained. "I would've tackled Berg if the whistle hadn't blown."

During the practice session the following Monday, Coury pulled out a cigar box full of rabbit's feet, telling his players that "this is what (Pasadena, the upcoming semifinal opponent) thinks of you."

Patton said that right after the Monarchs had beaten Pasadena, 28-13, the opposing head coach, the late Tom Hamilton, who always was regarded as an accomplished coach and nice-enough man in the same vein as Coury, came in to the winning locker room to congratulate the Monarchs. "I knew then that there was no way this guy would pull that sort of thing," Patton said, adding that Coury had produced the ploy on his own to motivate his players, just as Enriquez had done two years previously with the sophomores.

Preparing for that '65 championship season, it seems the brainy Coury always was mentally advanced of his coaching counterparts in innovations. For instance, in Obbema's junior year, the Monarchs, who hadn't allowed single point all season, lost to archrival Servite and finished 9-1, being denied a playoff berth by virtue of the lone loss.

Keeping one step ahead of opponents, Coury convened a week-long, between-season camp, at Chapman College in nearby Orange; it included grueling, two-a-day drills in the summer heat and requiring players to live all week in college dormitories. However, what really made the biggest impression on movie-buff Obbema and his teammates was celluloid in nature.

"Every night, we would watch the Servite game on film," Patton said, indicating that Coury – and Patton's Notre Dame's coaches, Head Coach Ara Parseghian and offensive coordinator Tom Pagna – had the most profound effect on how he molded his own coaching philosophy. "It was by example, not just a single thing."

Patton said the Servite game film was repeated nightly so that the idea it would not happen again was ingrained in the players' minds. Obviously, it worked, with the evidence being the 1965 season that ensued.

"Dick Coury was well ahead of his time; he was organized and was a great coach," Pultorak said. In fact, Coury involuntarily and inadvertently shared a nickname with Obbema: Big O. The reason? "I remember when I was a sophomore, we had seven shutouts in eight games," so the 'O' really stood for 'zero.' "Coach was a defensive genius," Pultorak said.

The 245-pound tackle, who got even bigger in college, said that for years, Coury would have Mater Dei players chant, "Every day, in every way, we get better and better."

Coury was so proud of how tough his teams were defensively that "whenever we had points scored on us, on the following Monday we ran 100 yards in practice for every point scored" by the last previous opponent, the veteran coach said.

Heisman winner John Huarte said it was invaluable taking lessons learned from Coury to Notre Dame, where he played first under Hughie Devore, then Parseghian.

Huarte termed Coury as "discipline-minded. He was a very good teacher and good communicator. You knew exactly what was expected of you" regardless of what position one played. Huarte said Coury was the total head coach. "We always had a strong defense, and the running game complemented the passing." Plus, Coury emphasized special teams and had an interesting bag of so-called "gadget" plays.

"Coach Coury always was very uplifting and treated (all) players with respect. He was totally dedicated, year in, year out, to his players improving. It wasn't just a seasonal thing," John Huarte said.

Toby Page, the quarterback who later was Obbema's USC teammate, also played one year with him at Mater Dei, when Obbema was a sophomore. That was 1963, as Mater Dei did not lose in the regular season and therefore was bumped up to the largest-schools classification for the postseason.

"We lost to Redlands in the first round. It was on the weekend that JFK (President John F. Kennedy) was shot," Page said, emphasizing that the Nov. 22 assassination of the nation's first Catholic president more negatively affected players

from a Catholic school than it did public-school
Redlands.

Although, like several of his star players,
Coury left Mater Dei for USC, Morgan said that the
Mater Dei Quarterback Club was created because of
the veteran coach's presence, enabling funds raised
from the effort to provide a perpetual scholarship
avenue for deserving students. Today, the club,
ramrodded by former Monarch player Tom Haupert,
takes advantage of the largesse of more than 30,000
Mater Dei alumni around the world.

Coury likes the idea that he is able to huddle
with 70 to 80 of his former players several times a
year, when possible, to continue the camaraderie.
The way the ex-players truly respect their former
coach, far beyond their playing days, is a direct
byproduct of Coury's long-held philosophy: "You
treat people the way you want to be treated – like
anything in life."

With all the positives the 1965 Monarchs
achieved because of exceptional talent, excellent
coaching and sometimes just plain luck, the real key
to the team's success may have been the Morgan
twins' mother. Every week she cooked a pre-game
meal at which Obbema would join the Morgan

family as sort of an honorary family member in their Tustin home, and every week they won – save the disputed St. Paul tie.

Because he achieved a high score on the Scholastic Aptitude Tests, Obbema, by virtue of that, coupled with his football talent, had his choice of where he would attend college.

The months before he made his ultimate decision were dotted with expenses-paid trips to virtually every part of the country – where he was wined and dined by many major-college programs.

He admits that if there was some way to make his recruitment process a permanent daily event, he would not mind because of the way highly prized prospects were always given the red-carpet treatment in those bygone days. And what teen-age boy would not relish the idea of being the honored guest at a nightly party after being reminded repeatedly during the day as to how his services were so desirable?

Eventually, though, Obbema felt compelled to choose USC. After all, there already was a built-in comfort zone with his high school head coach and several former teammates having opted for the Troy route. Therefore, from that point forth, for the rest of his life, Joe Obbema would be bleeding only cardinal and gold – that is when he was not shedding blood from numerous surgeries.

9

POP GOES THE WARNER

The identity crisis . . . occurs in that period of the life cycle when each youth

must forge for himself some central perspective and direction, some working

unity, out of the effective remnants of his childhood and the hopes of his

anticipated adulthood.

-- Young Man Luther (1958), Ch. 1, Erik (Homburger) Erikson (1902-1994)

As an aspiring athlete on the cusp of being a teen-ager who was generally bigger and better than most of his youthful teammates, Joe Obbema had quite a legitimate claim to donning a Superman uniform that was popular with boys in the 1950s and '60s.

Whether he actually wore the get-up or not is not important, however; he did not need a cape with an "S" emblazoned on the chest to perform some of the feats on the football field that others witnessed with awe.

The *milieu* was an activity called Pop Warner, and Buena Park was not unlike most other U.S. suburbs during an era when such movements continued to grow. The city of then-roughly 30,000 people straddled the Santa Ana Freeway (Interstate 5) about 20 miles southeast of downtown Los Angeles. It was home to a burgeoning Western village-turned-major theme park, Knott's Berry Farm, birthplace of boysenberry pie and popular fried-chicken dinners. But it also was just five miles from the still-fairly new prototype for *all* such ventures, Disneyland, in neighboring Anaheim.

While there was an upscale area still in the early growth stages on the city's northern tier, Belhurst Estates, which ringed the new Los Coyotes Country Club north of the freeway, most of Buena Park was populated by middle-class families, both white-collar and blue-collar. The heads of household – usually still the fathers in those *Leave It To Beaver* days – typically earned their weekly paychecks mainly in nearby aerospace factories, the giant Hunt's vegetable processing plant in neighboring Fullerton, sales jobs or maybe in the numerous other manufacturing facilities in Orange or Los Angeles counties. The Uniroyal Tires "castle" 11 miles to the northwest was where George Obbema, Joe's father, worked.

If you drove far enough south – about 15 miles – on the city's main north-south thoroughfare, Beach Boulevard (California Highway 39), you would wind up smack-dab in the Pacific Ocean at Huntington Beach, known popularly as "Surf City." Following Highway 39 due north would take you into the imposing San Gabriel Mountains 30-plus miles away; the often-snowcapped peaks like Mount Baldy were visible from Buena Park on clear days, which were becoming increasingly rare because of the encroaching, choking, infamous Southern California smog.

None of these nuances seemed to bother the Pop Warner League's Falcons, who had their collective eyes trained on starring someday perhaps at one of the two big universities in the Southland, USC and UCLA.

"I was 11 years old when we had our first full-contact tackle scrimmage," said Obbema, who actually *did* achieve the college dream, playing on a consensus national championship team for the

University of Southern California Trojans less than a decade after that initial Pop Warner scrimmage.

Pop Warner football, something akin to baseball's Little League, was officially the Pop Warner Conference. Named after legendary college coach Glenn S. "Pop" Warner, who reputedly invented modern football, it began in Pennsylvania in 1930. It allowed boys between the ages of 10 and 13 to enjoy team-style camaraderie while preparing them to play higher-level football, according to conference literature published in game programs in 1960.

According to the official literature, a Pop Warner bowl series was instituted with a more-elaborate bowl series added in 1948.

"National prominence came to the Conference with the first bowl game in 1948," the official version stated. "This was a contest between a Philadelphia team sponsored by Frank Palumbo, and a New York team sponsored by Frank Sinatra. The following year General Bob Neyland sent a team from the University of Tennessee area to Easton, Pa., for the second Bowl Game."

The attendant "world-wide publicity" resulted in a burgeoning trend, as an estimated 300 cities and towns nationwide had Pop Warner programs.

Pop Warner officials always have regarded the young teams not just as venues for playing football but as "youth festivals." Such was the case in both the fall of 1960 and 1961, when Obbema and the Falcons played in a series of postseason bowl games in and around Buena Park. The local games, in which the Falcons competed against worthy opponents from as far away as Texas, Louisiana and New York, were financially underwritten by the local chapter of an international service organization, the Buena Park Optimist Club.

Players had varying and gradated limits imposed on them as each season progressed – for minimum and maximum weight, playing time, team size and even the height of trophies winning squads earned. This was in a day when "false equality" and guaranteed outcomes for the sake of political correctness had not yet been imposed; in other words, only winning teams earned trophies, while the unfortunate losers went home hoping they would improve by next year.

In 1960, Obbema's first Pop Warner season, the Falcons competed in the Major-League Midget Division, wherein the heaviest weight in shorts was 110 pounds early in the season and 115 pounds for later games. The Buena Park team's 8-1 record was the best in the entire Orange County association, as the squad compiled 243 points while surrendering only 65. There were 16 teams in two divisions. The Falcons' only loss in the 1960-61 stretch was 7-0 to the Garden Grove Knights, which they later avenged.

The team was organized by a huge head coach, 6-foot-5, 270-pound Herb Wilson. He was assisted by Tom Davison and Jack Bighead. Bighead, a Native American who had been a track star at Pepperdine College, later coached at nearby Western High School but carried a Screen Actors Guild card and had appeared as "Little Boy" in *The Jim Thorpe Story* along with being a Paiute warrior in several episodes of the long-running television series *Bonanza*. The following year, Tom Hill was added to the volunteer coaching staff.

(Interestingly regarding Bighead having a role in the Jim Thorpe movie, the real Thorpe's most notable coach had been one Glenn S. "Pop" Warner at Carlisle Indian Industrial School.)

Although Superman analogies are apt, Obbema had other heroes, especially the most reputedly *macho* movie actor of all time, according to Marv "Tink" Hahn, who has been Obbema's best friend since they were youth-league teammates. Hahn's firsthand recollections of his friend's on-field and off-field feats are both legion and legend, as are Obbema's own remembrances.

"Joe thought he was John Wayne. One of the greatest plays I have ever seen was made by Joe in Pop Warner," said Hahn, who himself was an offensive tackle on Fullerton Junior College's 1965 Junior Rose Bowl champions before injuries ended his football aspirations. "We were trying to block a punt against a team from Utica, New York. It was fourth-and-43. Joe and I were in the middle (and) they had two blockers who stepped in front of the punter about five yards away.

"I elected to take an outside route, and as I was going around them, I saw Joe go flying overhead. He had stepped on the shoulder pads of the blockers, and they catapulted him as he extended (and) the bottoms of his feet were way above my head.

"He blocked the punt about 10 feet in the air with his stomach," Hahn said. It was young Obbema's 15th blocked kick that season.

At the ensuing awards banquet, former Wisconsin Badgers and Los Angeles Rams star Elroy "Crazy Legs" Hirsch was guest speaker. An astounded Hirsch told the assemblage as he narrated film highlights of the game that he never had seen a play like Obbema's – in the Big Ten, the pros, *anywhere*.

After the Falcons graduated to the Major League's highest division, the Bantams, in 1961, they were unbeaten and good enough to earn their way into two national bowl games that were played locally – the Nov. 25 Disneyland Bowl at Anaheim's La Palma Stadium and the Dec. 29 Berry Bowl at Buena Park High School.

Buena Park met its only previous conqueror from the year before, Garden Grove, for the Orange County Bantam title, and the Falcons won to avenge the previous year's loss and advance to a bowl game.

To say there is no crying in sports would be proven otherwise by Hahn, he himself admitted.

"I tended to play on emotion, and I often would literally be weeping on the sidelines waiting for the defense to go," Hahn said. "Somewhere around the first quarter, one of the assistant coaches noticed me crying and thought I was hurt. He said, 'What's wrong with Hahn? He's crying.'

"Joe interrupts him and says, 'Leave him alone; he plays better when he's crying.' We won the game, 14-13, and qualified for the Disneyland Bowl. Ronnie Brown and Joe stuck the ball-carrier, and I recovered the fumble to prevent the extra point, which was the difference in the game," said Hahn, now age 65, and a master electrician who is in charge of ensuring that a massive electrical grid in Northern California remains in optimum working order for the millions of people it serves. (Brown, incidentally, was a nephew of Obbema's high school head coach and college assistant coach Dick Coury and was from a neighboring family of 16 children that produced several football coaches itself.)

As had been the case over and over through the years, the initial time Hahn and Obbema met illustrates what those close to him know about Joe Obbema: A compassionate heart beats underneath an Armor-All veneer.

The first time Hahn and Obbema had ever noticed each other individually was in Pop Warner, and Herb Wilson was the coach. A teammate named Jimmy Castles had cerebral palsy, but it was not that noticeable.

"I pushed the kid, and he fell over backwards," Hahn said. "Joe saw that, and he got in my face," which was a bit forbidding since Obbema always was bigger than Hahn despite the former being younger by a few months.

As is often the case, Castles gained perhaps an unintentional bit of revenge later on their Pony League baseball team.

"He continued to improve with the use of his hands, even though he looked like he always limped," Hahn said of Castles. The two got sent down to the best team in the Pony League Minors, with (here is the justice) Castles batting eighth and Hahn ninth.

Then, Hahn said, Castles got on base in one memorable game, and Hahn knocked him in with a home run.

Hahn never had a brother, but was the baby in his family following three older sisters.

"It's like I grew up with four mothers," he said. "So Joe and I were like brothers." Both got their respective nicknames in different ways. Hahn became Tink because he was called a "little stinker" as an infant, but one of his sisters could only say "Tink"; Obbema received his "Big O" moniker from a Santa Ana sportswriter while playing at Mater

Dei, utilizing the appellation to name a company he
later owned as Big O Transportation.

Hahn said Herb Wilson constantly referred to
young Obbema as "a Philadelphia lawyer" because
of his nit-picky emphasis on the most-precise
points. (Merriam-Webster defines the Philadelphia
practitioner as "a lawyer knowledgeable in the
most-minute aspects of the law.")

"When we were playing Pop Warner, some
guys had a weight problem at 125 pounds (the
Bantam limit) and some guys like Danny Young
(the most talented natural athlete on the team, who
could punt the ball 55 yards at age 12) and Ronnie
Brown" were among them, Hahn said. "Brown
shows up at practice with a black eye, and Herb
Wilson asks, 'Where did you get that?' And Joe
said, "I gave it to him because I saw him eating a
hot dog because he'd gain weight'."

When the Buena Park Falcons faced a
powerful, unbeaten team from upstate New York in
the 1961 Berry Bowl following the Disneyland
Bowl, the East Coast squad had several African-
American players. The cooperative aspect of the
Pop Warner credo preached that host teams would
invite the visitors to stay in local homes, and the

Obbema family was scheduled to have one of the young New Yorkers be their house guest.

The New Yorkers had seven or eight blacks on their team and, in those days, few black people lived in Buena Park, and none in the Obbemas' neighborhood at all.

"My brothers were only 4 and 2 years old, so my mother was trying to explain that this kid was black" to prepare them for their impending house guest, Joe Obbema said. "We had a mahogany, dark-colored chair," which Mrs. Obbema used to illustrate her point.

"She told them that we were going to have someone stay with us who was darker than that *dark brown chair.*

"The plane was late, so he didn't get there until 2 in the morning, and (the visiting player) turned out to be really dark. So Bobby, who was 4, turns to my mom and said, 'Mother, he's a lot darker than that chair.'"

The chair aside, the Falcons shut out the New Yorkers, 56-0, breaking a long winning streak that had stretched over several seasons, and sending the young man named Charlie back to upstate New York broken-hearted.

Much earlier than Pop Warner, Joe Obbema had begun showing tendencies that set him aside from the crowd:

Some examples from best friend Tink Hahn, courtesy of Obbema's late mother, Charline (who generally ruled her household with a typical iron hand – or two – with the butt-end of a broomstick to enhance her natural "touch"):

> -- "Joe said a swear word, so his mom went to wash his mouth out with soap. Joe took the bar away and ate it."

> -- "Joe was about 4 and got a new (tricycle) for Christmas. He did something bad so his mom hid the trike in the garage and told him Santa had taken it back. The next thing, she sees Joe walking down the street with a hammer in his hand. She asked him where he was going, and he said, 'I'm going to find that son of a bitch and get my bike back.'

> -- "When he lived in Norwalk before Buena Park, he had a friend named (for real) Tom Sawyer. Tom would often go find a guy that looked older and tell him (pointing to Joe), 'My friend says he can kick your ass.' Joe ended up in a fight which he would always

win and then would kick Tom's ass also." (So obviously this Tom Sawyer's sidekick *was not* exactly Huckleberry Finn.)

-- "His dad would take him into bars when he was a toddler and make bets how long he could hang on a broomstick supported between two bar stools. Joe would hang there indefinitely until dad took him down." (A version of this routine would be repeated, like-father-like-son, in later years when one of Obbema's college roommates, John G. Smith, accompanied Joe and the latter's eldest child, Matt, to the liquor store. "Joe would set Matt on the counter, then go back to the cooler to grab some beer, and nobody said anything about it," Smith said.)

That Joe Obbema played football after Pop Warner was remarkable, considering his actual medical condition. Nonetheless, he was forced to sit out football his freshman year at Mater Dei, in south Santa Ana, the Orange County seat, and 10 miles from his home.

"My doctor advised me that it would be a good idea to get out of football for good. I was devastated. I told the doctor to go to Hell," Obbema said of what was diagnosed as osteochondritis. It was a condition by which his right knee had grown too fast, forcing him to wear a cast over calcium deposits on the affected knee. "It looked like leprosy; it was awful," Obbema said, also discovering at the time that he was allergic to adhesive, causing him to use special socks, and adhesive-free gauze.

"When I worked out with the Mater Dei team in the summer between my freshman and sophomore years, the orthopedic surgeon diagnosed a fixed lumbar vertebrae pinching on my sciatic nerve, and I cursed at him when he recommended that I (no longer) play football. My mom got really mad at me," Obbema said.

Without telling anybody – and on advice from Mater Dei athletic trainer Joe Knapp -- he embarked on an intense, self-propelled rehabilitation program, learning an exercise known as a reverse sit-up.

"Joe Knapp recommended reverse sit-ups on the bench press," Obbema said. "I took a 10-pound weight, laid on my stomach (in a prone rather than the supine position normally associated with standard sit-ups), with half of my body hanging off the bench.

"It hurt like Hell," said Obbema. All those reverse sit-ups were responsible much later in life for surgeons having difficulty inserting screws in his back "because of really strong back muscles," he said.

After doing tons of reverse sit-ups daily, within a year, he got the go-ahead to return to the gridiron and became frankly one of the best players ever in one of the nation's most-storied high school football programs.

While not an individual who wears his faith on his sleeve, Obbema always has turned to prayer for solace and guidance. That was accelerated at one critical point in his life.

"I went to church daily, including Saturdays, in my senior year" at Mater Dei "until I got a scholarship" to USC, he said.

All that praying was not just that he merely be awarded a scholarship. Obbema was seeking Divine guidance to help him narrow his choices that were piled in a couple of shoe boxes full of invitation letters and telegrams from many of the nation's elite Division I football programs. With his 1,300-plus score on the Scholastic Aptitude Tests, he could go anywhere he wanted. Yet he chose USC, of course.

In the summer between Mater Dei and USC, he culminated his prep career by being selected to play in the Orange County All-Star game.

Coury, Obbema's longtime mentor to whom he has remained like a son over the years, said that, long after football had ended, Obbema was part of a generous and grateful gesture in 2009 courtesy of the Mater Dei Lettermen's Club.

"The thing I can relate to regarding Joe, he came down from Las Vegas to my 80th birthday party," Coury said of the Orange County get-together organized by former Monarch players Dick "Litz" Litzinger and John Heffernan, with another ex-Mater Dei player, Eric Patton, serving as unofficial host near his southern Orange County home and school where he coached and taught English.

Forty of Coury's former Monarchs showed up to honor the veteran coach. "Things like that, I get tears talking about it . . . some of the other things you don't see that carry onto the football field. I love the guy," Coury said of Obbema.

Although when high school started, Obbema, Tink Hahn and another boyhood buddy named Steve Sturm physically went their separate ways – Obbema to his parochial school, Hahn to Western High and Sturm to Buena Park High – they somehow still managed to stick together whenever possible.

"We had kind of become a kind of Three Musketeers," Hahn said. "We saw each other a lot despite going to different high schools" that competed in three different leagues – the Monarchs in the Angelus, Western's Pioneers in the Sunset and Buena Park's Coyotes in the Freeway. "We all had cars anyway; before that, it was bikes."

The Three Musketeers sometimes conspired to shake up things for those around them, not unlike the Alexandre Dumas fictional trio of Porthos, Athos and Aramis.

"We had an apartment at a place called the Continental Fullerton on the third floor," Hahn remembered. "Obbema came in to a party while Steve Sturm was sitting with his girlfriend on the couch. Joe started yelling at Steve, 'You son of a bitch,' just really screaming."

Sturm played along and started pleading with Obbema, "No, no, no, please don't hurt me!" Then the fake tormentor grabbed him and dragged him out onto the balcony. Obbema then picked up Sturm over his head like a barbell – the way a pro wrestler like Matt Obbema might do -- and pretended to throw his "victim" off the third-floor balcony.

Perhaps this is why Joe Obbema always regarded pro wrestling as contrived.

"Steve holds on to the handrail, and Joe doesn't let go of Steve. Everyone in the apartment except me is screaming, especially the girls -- maybe 25 people," Hahn said. "The first time was extemporaneous, then they started doing it on a regular basis, until it no longer drew screams. They would come back in laughing with their arms on each other's shoulders."

(Today, Sturm owns and operates a company called Bore-Max, Hydraulic Elevator Parts, so apparently the "lift" he got from good buddy Obbema had a profound effect on him and his choice of a livelihood.)

Hahn always has been adept at producing yet another story, especially with Joe Obbema at the center. Interesting thing is, though, while

embellishment often plays a role, the stories Hahn
tells about Obbema *never* have to be made up.
There always seems to be someone, somewhere,
who can easily corroborate the tales.

"The night Joe signed his letter of intent, we
went to three parties, and he kept pulling the plug,
worrying about getting in trouble. Never mind that
he had gone to wild recruiting trips and did
many (unorthodox and potentially illegal) things
over the last several weeks," Hahn relates.

"At one point, I had two telephone operators
in a bedroom waiting for Joe to come back. When I
finally left to find him, they left also. He found a
girl on the corner . . . having a b-day party and
invited us -- all girls, except for a few guys. I had a
girl on each arm and a beer in each hand seeing
which girl could get the closest; Joe got nervous, so
we left."

That was a good thing, Hahn said, because
they found out later all the girls from that party went
skinny-dipping around midnight, and the police
came, plus the girls were probably under-age.

The irrepressible Hahn wasn't done, however.

"We went to another party where I was
putting moves on a girl from Western (Hahn's alma
mater), no name required," he said. "She thought I

was Dick Hough (Hahn's Junior College All-America quarterback teammate at Fullerton Junior College who had played for Western's bitter archrival, Anaheim), and I didn't discourage that thought. OK, I lied; I said I was Hough.

"Again, Joe got nervous, and so we left. Of all the blatant things he did, Joe was very meek that night."

When Orange County still had plenty of its namesake citrus fruits actually growing there, the social/recreational opportunities abounded.

"Joe's old Mater Dei friends rented an old orange grove house in the middle of nowhere; many animal-type parties happened there," Hahn said.

With marriage, divorce, kids and eventual moves out of California, it was many years before Hahn and Obbema saw each other in-person again. Until recently, they lived only a few miles from each other in Las Vegas.

"In the '90s, I got back in touch with him -- I was back in California after 17 years in Washington state," Hahn said. "When I came back, I looked him up at his Buena Park house" where Obbema lived

with Linda, his second wife, and their blended
family.

All along, it was the memories, not just the
physical presence, which bound together these two
rollicking buddies.

Hahn, coming off his junior college
championship at Fullerton, wanted to be a
Trojan,too, but two different knee injuries – one at
age 16 at Western, the second at Fullerton –
prevented him from going any further.

"But I don't dwell on it," he said. He would
rather conjure up the good old times with his best
friend, even when it created occasional momentary
fear.

"He and I got an apartment once in Fullerton
in '67 to defray our costs. They had this party room
and you rented it out," Hahn said. "I went off with a
girl for about an hour and a half and, when I came
back, the place was all torn up and there was a
drunk guy tearing the sink off the wall. There was a
blood trail when the guy's buddy dragged him off,"
still alive but worse for the wear.

Obbema then turned to Hahn with a fretful
voice and said, "Oh, no, I killed him!"

Again, it was simply Joe Obbema being himself one more time – protecting someone else's property, or honor, and using his fists to do it.

Joseph J. Obbema got to where he is now by practicing a simple dictum:

"You go through life, and you have a lot of acquaintances and a few friends. When you're willing to do things for people, it works vice-versa. And another thing (similar to how Winston Churchill exhorted fellow Britons during World War II's darker days): Never, ever give up – on anything in life."

ONCE A TROJAN, ALWAYS A TROJAN

<u>EPILOGUE</u>

The one constant that has prevailed throughout Joe Obbema's life – other than the gold 1967 national championship ring with the cardinal stone encased in it that he never removes – is his willingness to help someone else.

While this applies to just about anyone, whether it involves someone he never had known previously, it certainly is pertinent when it comes to family members. It is precisely for that latter reason that Joe and Linda Obbema permanently left Las Vegas, Nev., where they had resided since the early 1990s, to live northeast of Austin, Texas, just after New Year's 2010, ultimately finding their new home in the small community of Taylor. A quick walk around their home reveals the multitude of Linda's artistic touch – from drawings and paintings she has created, to handmade pieces of various-sized furniture and holiday decorations crafted by this ingenious woman.

Now that they are in Central Texas, they are able to be near some of the children and grandchildren in their blended family that has developed in their quarter-century of marriage. This is especially true regarding 18-year-old grandson Dayne Bullock, who is a promising, 6-foot-4, 245-pound ambidextrous long-snapper and offensive tackle at Westwood High School in Austin, the Texas state capital. Joe Obbema was good enough to have earned a full athletic scholarship at the University of Southern California more than four decades ago, and now, it is in his blood and bones that he bears what he feels is a special responsibility to be there day-to-day for Dayne.

Not everyone who plays football can do what Dayne does, and as well as he does it. Long-snappers, incidentally, are those valuable rare-birds in the sport: They possess the innate ability to accurately whip the football through their legs in a perfect spiral, while their head is upside-down and looking backward, some 7-14 yards to a place-kicker and holder, or a punter, who anxiously await the snap. It is a gridiron "art form" so precise that, Dayne's current head coach filmed his prodigy for college recruiters, and it paid off, as Dayne will be headed in fall 2013 to Southern Baptist University on an athletic scholarship. Being able to snap the ball back equally well with either hand certainly is a bonus for Dayne Bullock.

While sixty-something Joe Obbema was not a long-snapper himself, when he was asked if he somehow senses a replication of his youthful self in young Dayne, Obbema replied, "He's something special," the same phrase used regarding young Joe Obbema by his legendary high school coach, Dick Coury, back in the mid-1960s. Therefore, Grandpa has been there firsthand the past three years to watch this budding star become something even more special. And while he is doing that, despite certain physical limitations, he is available to help anyone else – just as has been the case all of Joe Obbema's life.

NOTES/SOURCES

CHAPTER 1

SI Vault, *A Man in Motion Beats Texas,* Oct. 2, 1967

USC Football Official Website, 1967 and 1968

Associated Press, *Ex-USC Football Player Goux Dies,* July 28, 2002

mapquest.com, updated January 2010

SI Vault, *If It's 1985, This Must Be Portland,* Feb. 25, 1985

SI Vault, *Animal's Coming Out of the Woods,* April 16, 1984

heisman.com, Heisman Trophy Official Website, Jan. 6, 2008

O.J.: The Education of a Rich Rookie by O.J. Simpson with Pete Axthelm, The Macmillan Company, 1970

CHAPTER 2

fanbase.com, 2009

The Tidings, Los Angeles Archdiocese newspaper, *Grady Resigns After 29 Years Leading Loyola Football*, March 11, 2005

GoVandals.com, University of Idaho Official Athletic Website, date indeterminant

The Oregonian, *Handling Heat A Constant for OSU's "Great Pumpkin"*, Oct. 23, 2003

Nevada Offender Tracking Information System, Offender Detail Record, Dec. 5, 2008

Justice Court Documents, Clark County, Nev., Sept. 18, 2007

Los Angeles Daily News, *Birmingham Looks Back at Glory Year*, November 16, 2000

The College Football Encyclopedia, Revised 2010

CHAPTER 3

Los Angeles Times, *Trojans Pull Out Showdown with UCLA*, Nov. 19, 1967

USC.edu, University of Southern California website, 2009

The Heisman by Bill Pennington, ReganBooks, 2004

CHAPTER 4

Menu, Julie's Restaurant, 1990

The Dallas Morning News, *Broadcast Beat: 'Brian's Song' Superior Film*, Nov. 27, 1971

Los Angeles Times, *Julie Kohl, 98, owner of Diners Near USC*, Jan. 16, 1902

Trojan Chronicle, *Julie's Trojan Barrel Closes*, Nov. 1, 1999

New York Times, *Football Pioneer Builds Big Men for Steelers*, Jan. 23, 2009

Sports Illustrated, *They Said It*, Sept. 5, 1977

CHAPTER 5

publicartinla.com, website, Photo of Statue of "The Wild Bunch", 2002

cui.edu, Concordia University Master's Program website, 2008

Jet, *Newspaper Discloses O.J. Simpson's First Wife, Marguerite, Was Never Abused*, July 18, 1994

Rockcitynews.com, *Welcome to El Porto*, 2009

Quarry FoundationWebsite, *Robert's Blog*, 1999

Los Angeles Times, Letter to the Editor: *Generation Gap at the Beach*, Aug. 26, 2006

Los Angeles Times, *Flip Flops, Meet Prada*, Aug. 3, 2006

fodors.com, *Great Mexican Restaurant Near L.A. or Manhattan Beach*, Dec, 8, 2008

The Cisco Kid Summary, Classic TV Series, March 20, 2009

U.S. Department of Commerce, Demographic Statistics, 2009

CHAPTER 6

Los Angeles Times, *L.A. Express to Play Portland in USFL Exhibition at Pierce*, Jan. 23, 1985

The Atlantic Philanthropies, *Stephen McConnell Appointed to Advocacy and Policy Post with The Atlantic Philanthropies Ageing Program*, June 9, 2008

S.A.F.E. Golf Tournament Statistics, 1990-2000

Sports Illustrated, *Woe, Be Gone*, Feb. 2, 2009

Los Angeles Times, *Name Was Synonymous with Trojan Football*, Oct. 5. 2008

New York Times, *Bob Chandler, Football Player*, *45*, Jan. 28, 1995

O.J. Simpson.info/the chase, website, date indeterminant

Sports Illustrated, *The NFL's Dirty Dozen*, Oct. 26, 1998

The Bantam Medical Dictionary, Revised Edition, March 1990

CHAPTERS 7 & 8

placesearth.com, Uniroyal Tires history, updated April 18, 2008

materdei.org, Mater Dei High School website, updated Jan. 2010

Phoenix Mercury team website, Sept. 12. 2006

CHAPTER 9

Pop Warner Conference Bowl Game Programs, 1960-61

collegefootball.org, Glenn S. "Pop" Warner Biography, date indeterminant

Los Angeles Herald-Examiner, *Fullerton in 201-5 Win*, Dec. 16, 1965

ACKNOWLEDGMENTS

I extend my most heartfelt thanks and appreciation to Joe Obbema for being so patient and diligent in enduring this project. Plus, an extra bouquet is tossed Linda Obbema's way for putting up with Joe, and abiding with me, for that matter.

Extra-special recognition is due Marvelous Marv "Tink" Hahn for always believing this was a worthwhile and entertaining effort. And Steve Sinders deserves special mention for lending his technical expertise in finalizing this project.

To the dozens of present and former NFL coaches, former college coaches and players, and friends, family and ex-teammates of Joe Obbema, who were interviewed for this book, I say thank you so much.

The patient, knowledgeable staff at Amazon and Kindle Direct Publishing must be commended for guidance and offering modern publishing resources for any author.

Maria Ross obviously has a very special place in my heart and I would be nothing without her love and support.   – PHIL ROSS

ONCE A TROJAN, ALWAYS A TROJAN

ABOUT THE AUTHOR

Phil Ross has more than 30 years' award-winning experience as a sportswriter, news editor and reporter, and editorial page editor on daily newspapers and in public relations. He has worked on daily newspapers in California, Nevada, Texas and Colorado, including *the Anaheim Bulletin, Orange Coast Daily Pilot, Ventura County Star-Free Press, Daily Commercial News, Las Vegas Review-Journal, El Paso Times* and *Daily News-Press*. Ross served five years as communications officer for the Colorado House of Representatives. He earned a degree in Mass Communication from Cal State Hayward (now Cal State East Bay) and is an honorably discharged Vietnam Era veteran of the U.S. Army. In addition to covering everything from high school sports to pro football, he also worked as a freelancer on the professional rodeo circuit, including covering the National Finals Rodeo. He also was a college and high school baseball umpire for 18 years. He lives with his wife in Denver.

"Once A Trojan, Always A Trojan" uses continual visualization and motion to follow the Forrest Gump-like life of Joe Obbema, a teammate of O.J. Simpson, Simpson's fellow College and Pro Football Hall of Famer Ron Yary, Tim Rossovich and several other first-round NFL draft choices on the 1967 USC consensus national championship football team. The story stage is set during the championship season, and spins from three key games during that run, through the triumphs and tragedies in Obbema's life. Along the way, fueled by incredible minutiae, are humorous, tragic and action-packed moments, including Obbema's colorful and fight-dominated sidelight as a bouncer while studying for his teaching certificate. Many never-before-published recollections and recountings surrounding famous game moments are captured, including first-hand interviews with several former NFL head coaches and college teammates who have been Obbema's lifelong friends, and those of the longtime "Voice of the Trojans," Tom Kelly. Using all the twists and turns of Obbema's journey as a springboard, the book is not merely a story about a successful football career that was shortened by injuries, but is designed to illustrate how it relates to life in general.

CPSIA information can be obtained at www.ICGtesting.com
Printed in the USA
BVOW02s2003160414

350862BV00012B/387/P